FROM GAMES OF GOD TO BUBBA'S FIELD:

A CENTURY OF THE MODERN OLYMPIC GAMES, 1896 - 1996

By

EDD WHEELER

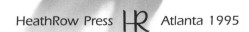

HeathRow Press HR Atlanta 1995

Book design by Gene Clopton
Drawings in text by Susanna Stevens
Drawings in Appendix by Margaret ReVille

Published by
HEATHROW PRESS
6467 Warren Drive
Atlanta, Georgia 30093-1114
770/447-9001 FAX 770/447-9005

LIBRARY OF CONGRESS
CATALOGING-IN-PUBLICATION DATA
From games of god to bubba's field: a century of the modern
    olympic games, 1896-1996
    by Edd Wheeler
        p. cm.
    Includes index
    ISBN 0-9648190-0-7

    1. Olympics – History.   I. Title.
    GV 721.5.W43   1995
    796.48 - dc 20   95-46631
                                      CIP

This book is licensed by the U.S. Olympic Committee. However, the conclusions and opinions herein are those of the author only and no official endorsement by the USOC should be inferred.

FOR ARTHUR BOLTON

who, denied the track, ran the swift race

CONTENTS

THE ONCE AND FUTURE GREATS *149*

A Personal Note by the Author

I do not know why man likes sport. Maybe for the same reason that the dog tosses his bone. Is it a statement of possession, amusement or boredom? The Olympics are, or could be, the highest expression of sport. At core, and in the nations, the Olympics test our bonds to earth and lift the fact that we are alive.

I recall that as a young man, between points at handball or racquets, I would revel at times in the basics of my sweat and for the briefest moment fix on the notion, a purposeful phantom, that my wrists were made of bronze and that I would live forever. It is less so now. I recall also that at the end, especially in victory hard come by, I felt elation but more a sense of loss. The contest had told me there were no more points to score. This is as it should be. This is as it has always been. Time eats us yet we remain hungry for the chase.

INTRODUCTION

The race is not always to the swift, but
that is where to look.
Hugh E. Keough

May God deny you peace
but give you glory!
Miguel De Unamuno

Chapter 1

AMBROSIA BECOMES BUBBA:
OLYMPIA TO HOTLANTA

It can be argued that the Olympic Games are going downhill. Born in ancient Greece at Olympia, mythological home of mighty Zeus and other gods well-fed on ambrosia, the Games move next to Atlanta, known affectionately and otherwise as Hotlanta, real home of Coca-Cola, where Bubba has been known to overfeed on pork rinds and barbecue.

Atlanta has hosted General Sherman and the NFL Super Bowl. But it has exhibited only marginal ability to channelize such events as "Freak-nik", an annual spring gathering of black college students. There are persistent questions about the city's capacity to pull off the 1996 Summer Olympic Games, the world's largest international festival.

Atlantans though seem confident of their place in sport's longest, most venerable procession. In this respect, Atlantans are like the self-assured boy in a schoolmaster story. When asked if he might be out of his depth, the boy quickly replied, "Perhaps but I can swim." There will be swimming in Atlanta. And about 25 other sports on the program for the centennial celebration of the Modern Olympic Games.

Bubba appears to be in high cotton and is preparing for the switch from barbecue to ambrosia.

Whatever the fare, a cardinal fact about the modern Games is that they draw spectators and produce records unimagined long ago. The Games have achieved something rare in history. They have lived up to their billing. Olympic athletes consistently have fulfilled the Olympic motto, *Citius, Altius, Fortius* (Swifter, Higher, Stronger). Records will fall briskly, even in the heat of

Atlanta, just as they fell in 1992 at Barcelona and in all preceding modern Summer Games.

But if the Olympics are about individual achievement, they are also about institutional protectionism. The Wide World of Sports is much like the rest of the galaxy. It is all about power, whether adorned with mystery or shorn of it. The Olympics are increasingly two-dimensional, with commerce spinning one axis and politics the other.

The first Olympic victor, the cook Coroebus, in ancient times ran for hometown and personal glory, while the 1996 Olympian, resplendently shoed, will sprint hardest for endorsements and more *bread* than ever imagined by the ancient Greek cook.

The Olympics have become both sport and spectacle, both games and glitz. The sacred competition, the Games of God, have evolved into Showtime, the stuff of Dream Team professionals, synchronized swimming and hot-dog somersaults on skis. The executive board of the International Olympic Committee has tentatively approved ballroom dancing as a demonstration sport in the future. Might stock car racing be just around the corner?

> *The executive board of the IOC has tentatively approved ballroom dancing as a demonstration sport. Might stock car racing be just around the corner?*

THE NEW PANTHEON IN DIXIE

The road leading to the new pantheon in Dixie has been an amazing one. The first 13 Olympian Games consisted of a single event, a sprint of just over 200 yards. Eventually some 24 ancient Olympic contests were featured. The first modern Games (Athens, 1896) awarded championships in only 11 sports categories: track and field events, gymnastics, wrestling, pole-climbing, lawn tennis, fencing, rifle and revolver shooting, weightlifting, swimming, the Marathon race and bicycle racing.

There were 223 events at the 1984 Los Angeles Games and 257 at Barcelona in 1992. The 1996 Atlanta Games plan some 269 contests.

Women have figured importantly in these increases. Women in

*Atlanta's new Olympic stadium will cost over 1400 times the tab
for the first Modern Olympic stadium in Athens.*

ancient Greece were forbidden participation in the Olympics but
those unmarried were allowed as spectators. Women competed
instead in the Games of Hera, a series of footraces by age category for unmarried girls. These exclusions probably trace back
to the role of virgins in the dimly revealed religious festivals pre-
dating the first recorded Games. Married women were excluded
from the Olympics under penalty of death. One matron from
Rhodes is said to have disguised herself as a trainer to her son, a
boxer. In excitement at his Olympic victory, she leaped over a
barrier to embrace him, accidentally exposing herself. She
escaped punishment only because she belonged to a family of several famous Olympians.

Eleven women participated in the second modern Games
(Paris, 1900). The Atlanta Games will feature over 3600 women
athletes, participating in all Olympic sports except boxing,
wrestling, weightlifting and modern pentathlon. Baseball for men
will see its counterpart, women's softball, appear for the first time
as an Olympic sport in Atlanta.

From representing less than one percent of Olympians in turn-
of-the-century Paris, women now account for more than a third
of modern Olympians. Gender equity may soon call for the addi-

tion of modern pentathlon (shooting, swimming, fencing, riding and cross-country running) or even weightlifting for women. Given the temper of the times, boxing or wrestling could even appear on a future hit list, depending upon where one separates gender equity from gender mania.

The earliest modern Games did not always feature the world's most distinguished athletes. A dour Englishman observed of the inaugural modern Games of 1896:

> Great Britain took little direct interest in the occasion and was inadequately represented, but the United States sent five men from Boston and four from Princeton University, who, though none of them held American championships, succeeded in winning every event for which they were entered. The Marathon race of 42 kilometers (26 miles), commemorative of the famous run of the Greek messenger to Athens with news of the victory of Marathon, was won by a Greek peasant.

However, it was not long before the Modern Olympics became showcase for the world's best in their trips through "the thrill of victory and the agony of defeat." Soon to form were the columns of superlatives, the "Peerless Mel" and "Peerless Paavo", the Flying Finns and the World's Fastest Human. In Olympic track-and-field championships since 1896, Olympic records have fallen in about 55% of final events. Every Modern Olympics after 1896 has produced at least one world record in track and field. More astounding, world records have been broken in 40% of Olympic finals in men's swimming events. See the **Appendix** (A.8).

Some improvements have been more dramatic than others. For example, early Modern Olympic records in the pole vault, shot put and discus have been obliterated. In other events, human physiology dictates that improvement must come by increment. Nowhere has improvement in the margins been more obvious than in sprint events.

Every Modern Olympics after 1896 has produced at least one world record in track and field. World records have been broken in 40% of Olympic finals in men's swimming events.

The first Olympian Games were held in 776 B.C., "and there is reason to believe that this is an exact date, the first fixed date in Greek history." The Games consisted of a simple foot race straight down the stadium at Olympia for a distance of about 210 yards. The first champion was Coroebus of Elis, a cook. His victory of course was not clocked, but there are reasons to believe that the time was somewhat less than 25 seconds, a time comparable to what might be expected today of a decent high school sprinter.

The winning time in the first 200-meter dash of the modern Games (1900) was just over 22 seconds. The winning time in the Atlanta Games probably will be slightly under 20 seconds. It likely will be run by an American superlatively trained, conditioned and equipped and running on a state-of-the-art track.

The early Greek athlete on average was about five and one-half feet tall, at least six inches shorter than his modern, more powerful, better trained Olympic counterpart. Yet the difference in their performance, over the course of 200 yards and 2800 years, is only about 20%.

Contemporary sprinters unquestionably are faster than their predecessors but not overwhelmingly so. Only incremental gains are possible over relatively short distances. And neither trainer nor Nike can put in what God left out. Man's evolvement as an innovator in technique and equipment has been more rapid than the evolvement of the human body.

But there obviously are enormous differences between the original Games, even the first modern Games, and those of today. The first foot race at Olympia likely drew only a few dozen serious contenders from the villages of the district of Elis in southern Greece. Probably no more than several hundred people, seated on the grassy slopes of the hill of Kronos, attended the one-day event. Later, as many as 40,000 spectators would watch the Games at Olympia.

The 1896 Athens Games were held in the rebuilt Panathenaic stadium for 45,000 spectators. Just over 300 athletes from 13 countries participated.

By contrast, the dashes in Dixie will be run in a new 85,000-seat Olympic stadium, erected at a cost of over $210 million. The Atlanta Games will attract more than 10,000 athletes from almost 200 countries. During two weeks of competition, some two-thirds of the world's population, about three billion people in all, will tune in as TV spectators.

The Atlanta Games have sprung forth, not quite full-grown except in tongue and grin, from the forehead of one whose name bespeaks Southern style followed by effort, Billy Payne. His industry and vision assembled the messengers who garnered the 1996 Summer Games for Atlanta, making it only the third American city ever to host the Summer Olympics. St. Louis hosted the 1904 Games and Los Angeles followed in 1932 and again in 1984.

The logical and sentimental favorite for the Centennial Olympics was Athens. Detractors of Athens pointed with deft, and blurring, hand to the city's deficient "infrastructure". But the real reason for choosing Atlanta may have been tied more to ethnic structure than to urban infrastructure.

It was soon apparent that the wide representation of non-Western persons on the International Olympic Committee considered themselves in no way within the shadow of the Acropolis. They felt more connected to the points pitched by Andrew Young, the former United Nations ambassador, and by Maynard Jackson, Atlanta's mayor at the time. Afro-American in this instance registered as a more relevant hyphenation than, say, Greco-Roman.

In today's Athens, Atlanta is known as "the city that stole our Olympics". The old order changes — in hue and cry, in color and texture.

RITUAL, COMMERCE AND THE LITTLE BARON

Both ritual and commerce attend the Modern Olympics. In July 1996, the president of the United States, answering to modern ritual and the opportunities of an election year, will open the Centennial Games in Atlanta. Trumpets will sound and cannons boom. Released white pigeons will crowd the skies. Thousands of athletes will parade in tightly choreographed patterns of color and display. Widespread splendor will cascade over occasional fragments of irony.

The Olympic flag will be hoisted, its five rings of blue, yellow, black, green and red burnished against a white background. The flag's bonding circles symbolize the unity of athletes from the five continents. It first flew in 1914 over the headquarters of the International Olympic Committee in Paris, in the same season that Europe was beginning to come apart against the teeth of World War.

An American athlete bearing the Olympic torch, carried by thousands of runners who started from Olympia four weeks prior, will light the Olympic flame which will burn in the stadium throughout the two weeks of the Games. The ancient Greeks, of course, would have been puzzled by the notion of carrying a torch, in synchronized journey, halfway across the plains of Elis much less halfway round the world.

A U.S. Olympian will recite the Olympic oath composed by the founder of the modern Games, Pierre de Coubertin: "In the name of all competitors I promise that we will take part in these Olympic Games, respecting and abiding by the rules which govern them, in the true spirit of sportsmanship for the glory of our teams." The rules now include drug testing.

Commerce will play in the Atlanta Games along a broad periphery. A *Gone With the Wind* theme park will open in anticipation of two million visitors to the 1996 Games. Corporate sponsors of the Olympics will preen. Coca-Cola alone has paid $40 million for its corporate sponsorship. NationsBank, Visa, Home Depot and others will help to hinge the gates.

Juan Antonio Samaranch, president of the International Olympic Committee, sees in this process something akin to the natural order: "The Olympics would not exist today if it weren't for our partnerships with commercial enterprises." Some will argue that Mr. Samaranch would not exist today as Olympic chief without the sponsorship he enjoyed under the totalitarian rule of former Spanish dictator Francisco Franco. In any event, Mr. Samaranch's committee in 1993 sold the U.S. television rights for the Atlanta Games to NBC for $456 million.

It is questionable whether its founder would recognize the Modern Olympics. Baron Pierre de Coubertin (1863-1937) was born to nobility. He grew to maturity in an era of what he called "an unprecedented disaster", the French defeat by Prussia in 1870.

Receiving an early Jesuit education, Coubertin made reform his life's ambition. Just over five feet tall, he was an aspiring fencer but an athlete of no special competence. Coubertin's initial aim was to reform French education by promoting physical fitness among the country's youth. He wrote of "a religion of sport." Yet events abroad soon encouraged him to widen his thrust.

Heinrich Schliemann's famous search for Troy captured the imagination of Coubertin's generation. By 1880 German archeologists had excavated extensively at Olympia. Interest was widespread in the ancient Games. Why not recreate them? Coubertin, at 31, summoned an international conference at the Sorbonne in Paris. In 1894 the International Olympic Games Committee, headed by Coubertin, approved the rebirth of the Olympics in Games to be held at Athens in 1896.

Coubertin's vision was to build the character of the world's youth through physical culture and athletic competition. He preached the cleansing and ennobling effect of sport, which he called an "impassioned activity" and one in which "our body rises above its animal nature." Coubertin had an imperfect understanding both of ancient Greece and modern athletics. But impressed with athletic achievements as he interpreted them in England and America, he sought to revive the Games "since the hour had struck when international sport seemed destined once again to play its part in the world."

In many ways, Coubertin's world of sport was a kinder, gentler place than today's in-your-face athletics. Coubertin did not write the Olympic creed but it identifiably reflects his philosophy: "The important thing in the Games is not winning but taking part. The essential thing is not conquering but fighting well." As preached by the visiting Bishop of Pennsylvania, beneath the vast dome of St. Paul's Cathedral in London during the 1908 Games, "It is less important to win, than to compete."

The above sentiments are seldom heard today, or if expressed they are taken largely as window dressing. Opponents are objects to be blown away. The instant gesture of victory is a televised high-five or leering taunt.

However, some of Coubertin's ideas come down to us as dated, even embarrassing. In his dotage and last public statement, Coubertin praised the 1936 Olympics in Berlin as "grandiose" Games, staged with "Hitlerian strength and discipline", which had "magnificently served the Olympic ideal." Almost 30 years earlier, Coubertin had written that the revived Games would provide "the means of bringing to perfection the strong and hopeful youth of our white race, thus again helping towards the perfection of all human society." A commentator subsequently observed that "neither James Thorpe nor Jesse Owens was the athlete whom he had in mind."

Pierre and Marie de Coubertin. He died bankrupt and "one of the few Frenchmen left undecorated."

But Coubertin cannot be demonized as a racist. This fact is seen clearly in his response to the sad spectacle of the 1904 Olympics in St. Louis. The Games had an ugly side. They featured so-called Anthropological Days, events by aborigines imported for the parodying of certain competitions. In one event, for example, a pygmy heaved a weight the mock-Herculean distance of ten feet. One supposedly authoritative source reported: "The sports of the savages, among whom were

Coubertin's world of sport was a kinder, gentler place than today's in-your-face athletics.

American Indians, Africans of several tribes, Moros, Patagonians, Syrians, Ainus and Filipinos, were disappointing; their efforts in throwing the javelin, shooting with bow and arrow, weight-lifting, running and jumping, provided to be feeble compared with those of white races."

Against the above mindset, Coubertin's response was prophetic: "As for that outrageous charade, it will of course lose its appeal when black men, red men and yellow men learn to run, jump and throw, and leave the white man behind them."

The visionary occasionally exhibits a touch of the poet. Coubertin's poetic efforts were recognized, as part of the early Cultural Olympics, with the prize for literature at the 1912 Games in Stockholm. An excerpt from Coubertin's winning *Ode to Sport* will reveal the flavor to be more rocky road than vanilla:

> O Sport, delight of the Gods ... you are Beauty ... Justice ... Daring ... Honour! The titles you bestow are worthless save if won in absolute fairness and perfect unselfishness. Whoever succeeds in deceiving his fellows by some ignoble trick, suffers the share of it in the depths of himself and dreads the dishonorable epithet which will be coupled with his name ....

One gets the idea. The lines though hardly leap with Olympic greatness. They are not the stuff of sprint and adrenaline. The wonder frankly is that other works submitted evidently ran inferior to Coubertin's *Ode*. One might suspect favoritism in the judging, but the poem was submitted by Coubertin under two German pseudonyms.

At road's end, after the good fight and bad poetry, it could be said that a French academic, by effort and pluck, had awakened the Games from their long sleep of 1500 years. Yet the last days were not kind to Coubertin. He and his wife were reduced to living largely off the generosity of friends. At his death, Coubertin "was financially bankrupt and, in the words of a biographer, 'one of the few Frenchmen left undecorated.' " A year later, in 1938, the great heart of the little baron was removed fittingly and enshrined at Olympia.

REVIVAL AND GHOSTS

Buried in silence at Olympia also are the records of most of the thousands of champions whose feats over the centuries were witnessed there. No record by time, of course, survives for track events in the ancient Games. Running against a clock, even had one existed for sport, would have been a completely alien concept for the Greek athlete. To finish first and victorious was all that mattered.

However, at least some attention was given to measurement of distances in field events. Two alleged marks, for the discus and long jump, have come down to us. They of course are things of the shade. Even more remote and uncertain is an alleged record for a combined jumping event, which will be touched on below.

As for the discus and long jump events, there doubtless are substantial differences between present techniques and how the two events were performed in ancient times. The Greeks at times may have used a type of thong for the discus toss. In the long jump, the athlete apparently held a weight in each hand. It is unclear, though, whether the weights were dropped or if ancient rules allowed an extra step or jump. Nonetheless, rough comparisons are possible:

	Discus Champion	Long Jump Champion
Surviving Ancient Olympics Mark	Protesilaus 152 feet	Chionis of Sparta in 656 B.C. 23 feet, 1 3/4 inches
1896 Games Record	Robert Garrett of U.S.A. 95 feet, 7 3/4 inches	Ellery Clark of U.S.A 20 feet, 10 inches
Modern Olympics Record	Jurgen Schult of East Germany in 1988 225 feet, 9 inches	Robert Beamon of U.S.A. in 1968 29 feet, 2 1/2 inches

It is entirely possible that some performances by ancient Olympians exceeded those of athletes in the inaugural Games of 1896 and in other modern Games as well. Yet it also seems true that the best of modern Olympians have jumped at least 25% further and have thrown the discus almost 50% further than their known ancient counterparts.

The ancient mark for the long jump may not have been equalled in the 1896 Games, but it clearly has been bettered in all subsequent Olympics. The ancient mark for the discus appears not to have been bettered until the 1928 Games, yet too much should not be made of the evidence given apparent differences in tossing the old disk of stone or bronze and the modern one of wood and metal.

The revived 1896 Games were held in Greece. The original stadium at Olympia had been destroyed by erosion, earthquake and landslide. The Games therefore were scheduled for Athens, where the ancient Panathenaic stadium, less than a mile east of the Acropolis, was rebuilt through the generosity of Georges Averoff, a wealthy Greek merchant in Alexandria. The reconstruction price tag was a million drachmas (about $150,000 in current terms). An admission ticket to the Athens Games could be purchased for a drachma (about 16 cents).

The average ticket for a single event in the 1996 Centennial Games will be just under $40. While admission to the Olympics has increased about 250-fold, it now costs over 1400 times what it did in 1896 to build an Olympic stadium.

By comparison, the average ticket for a single event in the 1996 Centennial Games will be just under $40. While admission to the Olympics has increased about 250-fold during the past century, it apparently now costs over 1400 times what it did in 1896 to build an Olympic stadium.

On Monday, April 6th, 1896, a small, wiry Harvard dropout from south Boston, James Connolly, hopped, stepped and jumped his way down the Panathenaic stadium to become the first Olympic victor in 1503 years. His distance was 44 feet and 11 3/4 inches.

It is vaguely recorded that the great Chionis of Sparta "jumped 52 feet" in the 29th Olympiad (664 B.C.). This almost certainly was a triple or combined jump of some sort. Comparisons are risky but, if Chionis' mark is accepted as a triple jump, it is possible that an ancient Olympic mark was not bettered until the 1936 Games and the triple jump of Japan's Naoto Tajima, whose distance was 52 feet and 6 inches.

*Illustration of the 1896 Panathenaic stadium:
the finish in the Marathon race.*

The three marks cited above, and in fact all previous Olympic records in the triple jump, were eclipsed in the 1992 Games at Barcelona by Mike Conley of the United States. His jump was 59 feet and 7 1/2 inches, an impressive 33% improvement over Connolly's distance and almost 15% better than the probably over-stretched mark attributed to the legendary Chionis.

To compare is a human urge. Comparisons are comforting. They suggest a continuum and a continuance. If we factor for the past, perhaps the future will factor for us. Comparisons are a natural result of serious inquiry. They will be common throughout this book. Yet sometimes they are to be taken with a grain of salt. Possibly even a mound.

Who was the best, last season or a hundred past? How does today's champion compare with those of the last Olympics or the ancient Olympics? These questions tread uncertain ground. An Olympian competes not only within the fixed arena of his event but within the confines of a fixed time. His immediate competitors are live athletes waiting at ready within a breathing, often tumultuous venue. The dash to the finish is motivated not by history but by those who might be closing fast in the here and now.

It is difficult, therefore, to judge who was the greater Olympic track star, Carl Lewis of 1992 or Jesse Owens of 1936? The question may be skewed in more ways than one. For example, it is possible to judge Lewis to be the greater track star but to find Owens the more important historical participant in the Olympics. Both the questions and answers presume much. When they are projected into more distant eras, the problems multiply. In gauging our best against the champions of a generation ago, we encounter shadows. In gauging our best against occupants of many generations ago, we may encounter only ghosts or wisps of nothingness.

But the brush against ghosts in some ways is unavoidable. Institutions such as the Modern Olympics, in fact, do not arrive at centennial status without accumulating a share of ghosts, that is, memories or spirits which hang at the edges and haunt, for good or ill, the living procession. One of the ghosts in the Olympic rings of the Atlanta Games in 1996 will be the spirit of the Barcelona Games, called by Juan Samaranch, a Barcelonese, "the best Games in Olympic history." How will Atlanta compare? Another ghost in the centennial year will be that of Athens. Will Atlanta prove deserving of its selection over the might-have-been celebration in Greece, home of the Olympics and site of the first modern Games?

However, the presence of one ghost may be sensed more strongly than others. The ghost of Baron Pierre de Coubertin. The Games of his era have changed vastly. Few will contest that the Modern Olympics no longer are only about sport, if indeed they ever were. They are now also about entertainment, business, wealth, professionalism, politics, boycott and protest. One of the most controversial issues threatening at present to occupy part of center stage in Atlanta is the protest of women's rights activists, who demand that the more than 30 countries which ban female athletes should not be allowed to compete in the 1996 Games.

The activists argue that the ban amounts to a form of discrimination as loathsome as the racial discrimination which resulted in South Africa being kicked out of the Games from 1964 to 1992. Issues of merit, consensus and shrillness aside, it is certain that Coubertin would not endorse the proposed exclusion. "To officially proclaim any form of ostracism," he emphasized, "would be a rent in the Olympic constitution."

Southern folklore tells that, if one chances upon a spirit, the way to get past it is to ask simply what it wants. If the ghost of Coubertin in Hotlanta is asked what it wants in the centennial

year of his Games, it might well respond, I want my Games back! He cannot have them, though. They are no longer his. The modern Games have passed into a mythology as inspired and clouded as the one from which Coubertin recovered them.

James Connolly dropped out of Harvard to win the first Olympic crown in 1503 years.

Chapter 2

THE FIRST DOZEN CENTURIES

There was a time before our Age of Entertainment. Before Elvis, before television or the light bulb, and more than a thousand years before the invention of printing. This era in Greece was inhabited by people similar to us in many ways. They ate things like cheese and sesame rolls, and enjoyed a good time, especially sporting events and festivals. They got some things right and some wrong. The Olympics was one of the things they got right.

From the first ancient Games in 776 B.C., the Olympics were held every four years for 12 centuries. They survived wars, invasions, plagues, tyrannies and even the destruction of Greek liberty. The ancient Olympics outlasted the political and social systems that created them. But nothing lives forever. In 393 A.D., the Christian emperor in Rome, Theodosius I, ordered all pagan festivals to be closed. The great god Pan was dead — and so were the Games. There followed a sleep of 1500 years.

Imagine that the dozen centuries of ancient Olympic history and our own century of modern Games are added and seen as a single hour on a clock. Imagine too that the 1500-year interruption of the Olympics is similarly translated in terms of hours. This mythical clock began and ran for just over 55 minutes, until stopped by Theodosius. It remained silent for more than an hour and ten minutes. Less than five minutes ago, the remarkable timepiece began again with the first Modern Olympics in Athens. In a few seconds, the clock will chime in the 1996 Atlanta Games.

The ancient Games were dominated by professionals not amateurs. The professional was one who devoted himself virtually full-time to an activity and trained properly for it. An *idiotes* did neither. The Greeks had no specific word for amateur, but it is telling that the Greek term closest in meaning to amateur is that from which the word "idiot" has descended.

By contrast the Latin term from which amateur derives means "lover". The amateur supposedly engages in a pursuit simply for the love or enjoyment of it.

The Olympic professional came to be paid royally for his efforts. The earliest Games counted honors chiefly in terms of personal glory. But later festivals brought keen competition between cities, widespread professionalism and huge financial reward to champions. Some cities recruited athletes from other regions.

Fortunes were paid to victors. Two hundred years after the first Olympics, Solon in Athens sponsored legislation to *reduce* to 500 drachmas (five year's earnings of a workingman) the reward paid for Olympic victory by Athenians. Later, an Olympic winner was paid 30,000 drachmas by a city in Asia Minor merely for participating in the local games.

Olympic victory led to a place in human memory and to the table of the most illustrious. Winners at Olympia took free meals for life at the city hall, along with councilmen, ambassadors and other respected leaders. The walk on Easy Street by ancient Olympians was possible without assistance from Nike.

"ALWAYS TO BE THE FIRST"

Team sports were all but unknown in the ancient Games. Athletes competed as individuals and honor went only to winners. It was a man-against-man world. No revisionist history will make it otherwise. The Greeks counted victory and nothing else in the Olympics. The champion's reward of the wild olive wreath was the only thing that brought glory. Losers did not congratulate winners. Defeat, no matter how close the contest, brought shame.

What Homer described as the

The champion's reward of the wild olive wreath was the only thing that brought glory. Losers did not congratulate winners. Defeat, no matter how close the contest, brought shame.

The ancient stadium at Olympia, where Milo the Giant is said to have carried an ox on his shoulders to the delight of the crowd.

motivation of his heroes was the same urge that drove the Olympic athlete, "always to be the first and to surpass the others." The margin of victory was unimportant. A walkover was as good as a trouncing. The main thing, the only thing, was the championship. Vince Lombardi would have liked these people.

By the time Homer appeared on the written page (c.550 B.C.), the Olympic Games included some nine categories of events. The most ancient were the running events, followed in time by jumping, javelin, discus, wrestling, pentathlon, boxing, equestrian, and pankration events. These are to be seen not only as sport but also as preparation for combat and the defense as needed of one's city. The discus throw, for example, may have begun as a test of ability to hurl stones in combat. The javelin, in stadium or on the battlefield, was thrown using a thong to spin the projectile for added distance and accuracy. The pankration, a loosely controlled form of mayhem, was the equivalent of unarmed combat in game format. The race in armor was as readily the province of the soldier as the sprinter.

The Games, therefore, were sport, military training, and a chance for glory and personal fulfillment. Along with, of course, risk of humiliation or being maimed. Socrates, as Xenophon recalled, urged upon fellow citizens the more utilitarian side:

> It is part of his profession as a citizen to keep himself in good condition, ready to serve his state at a moment's notice. The instinct of self-preservation demands it likewise: for how helpless is the state of the ill-trained youth in war or in danger! Finally, what a disgrace it is for a man to grow old without ever seeing the beauty and the strength of which his body is capable!

Homer, who lived possibly a full century before the first recorded Olympics, mentions Games of five events: foot race, wrestling, jumping, discus and boxing. However, the first Olympics featured only the sprint. The other four events in Homer were added perhaps by reciters of the story by the time that someone finally recorded the epic in writing.

The ancient running events corresponded roughly to 200, 400 and 2000-meter races. The race in armor, introduced in the 65th Olympiad (520 B.C.), was the last event of the Games and was run on the afternoon of the fourth day. Later Games featured a relay torch-race of about 2500 meters, the ancestor of our modern relays and also, in much modified form, the modern torch procession bearing the Olympic flame. An expert reminds us that "the Marathon race was never heard of until modern times: the Greeks would have considered it as a monstrosity."

Jumping as sport was done in a manner strange to us. The athlete held a weight of about four pounds in each hand. The weights may have been dropped before landing. The Greeks, who knew little of physics or gravity, apparently had the curious notion that the weights would somehow assist in a longer jump.

Wrestling appeared in 708 B.C. as an Olympic sport. There eventually were two types, upright and ground wrestling. Victory was scored in upright wrestling by throwing the opponent to the ground. More violent was ground wrestling, which allowed grappling but not striking one's opponent until he admitted defeat by holding up a finger. The vulgar gesture of raising the finger as silent profanity may be an extension, er, corruption of this practice.

The pentathlon, also first mentioned at Olympia in 708 B.C., consisted of jumping, discus, javelin, foot race, and wrestling events. The victor may have been required to win at least three events, one of which had to be wrestling, the last sport held in the pentathlon. Some believe that the pentathlon was the most prestigious of Olympic events. That interpretation is consistent with the modern practice of often referring to the winner of the Olympic decathlon as the world's greatest athlete.

The pankration (648 B.C.) was a vicious sport. The contestants used free-for-all tactics from wrestling and boxing. Only gouging and biting were prohibited. A favorite opening was to break an opponent's finger. The wrenching of limbs out of socket was common. Death by strangulation was not unknown. The contest ended when one of the combatants admitted defeat by raising a finger. Assumedly not the one that may have been broken at the outset.

THE GREATEST OLYMPIAN?

The original Olympics were an all-Greek affair. For hundreds of years, only freeborn Greeks competed. The Olympics honored Zeus, king of the gods. Other major festivals were the Isthmian, Nemean and Pythian games. An illustration of the victory crowns awarded in the four ancient games can be found at the last page of the **Appendix** of this book.

The festival at Olympia held deep religious meaning until, in the second century B.C., Rome conquered Greece. Thereafter, Romans and others were allowed to compete in the Games. The festival in time took on more of the trappings of the ampitheater than the Games of God. Championships were had through money or intimidation. The emperor Nero in 65 A.D. was declared an Olympic victor in several categories. In one event, he was the winner in a field of one. The emperor simply forced opponents to withdraw.

But for every impostor there were hundreds of genuine champions in the history of the ancient Games. Some of their feats were so remarkable that they have passed into the region of legend. One of the earliest superstars was a wrestler of the sixth century B.C., Milo the Giant. He shunned the traditional athlete's diet of cheese, beans and water, concentrating instead on whole sides of meat garnished with hard exercise. The massive Milo was said to have carried an ox on his shoulders through the stadium at Olympia to the delight of the crowd. He and Hipposthenes won more consecutive athletic championships (six each) than any other Olympians in history, ancient or modern. It may have been partially for this reason that victory in wrestling was among the most coveted and respected of ancient Olympic crowns. Over a period of more than 20 years, Milo won wrestling championships six times at Olympia and six times as well in the Pythian Games.

Milo the Giant supposedly met his death not by clogged arteries from meat but by vanity in the forest. Legend has it that he came upon a tree which had been partially split by woodcutters. In proud gesture, he attempted to finish splitting the tree by brute force. The trunk, however, is said to have closed on his hand and thus trapped he was eaten by wolves.

Hipposthenes of Sparta won six consecutive Olympic victories in wrestling. His son, Etoimokles, won in the following five Olympiads. Their 40-year domination represents a dynasty that has no parallel in the history of sport.

Two other wrestlers must be considered among the greatest of Olympians. Hipposthenes of Sparta, as mentioned, won six consecutive Olympic victories. His son, Etoimokles, won in the following five Olympiads. Their 40-year domination represents a dynasty that has no parallel in the history of sport.

A boxer, Theogenes of Thasos, also has an impressive place as one of the foremost in the first rank of Olympians. He won three consecutive boxing victories at Olympia, as well as the championship in the pankration in a successive Games. Throughout the mid-fifth century B.C., Theogenes' athletic victories totaled more than 1300. He was a heavyweight in every sense. There being no divisions by weight, the athletically gifted giant prevailed.

Track stars too number among the ancient immortals. Astylos of Kroton won six crowns in three Olympiads in equivalents to the 200 and 400-meter events. Polites of Keramos, in the 212th Olympiad (69 A.D.), won three Olympic crowns in a single morning in foot races of 200, 400 and 2000 meters. These Greeks with difficult names left records easily understood by anyone with passing knowledge of the meaning of prevailing repeatedly in world-class competition, not just in a single Games but over a period of years.

Possibly the greatest ancient Olympian was Leonidas of Rhodes. In four consecutive Olympiads over the course of 12 years (164 to 152 B.C.), Leonidas won the 200 and 400-meter foot races as well as the race in armor. The latter, a great crowd pleas-er, covered a distance of either 400 or 800 meters. The evidence is uncertain. But what is clear is that Leonidas dominated Olympic track competition with a supremacy unknown before or since his time. Twelve Olympic crowns in all. He was the top Olympian, in events favoring youth and vigor, from young manhood to what must have been his late-thirties.

Leonidas' records were the ore of legend and myth. It is not surprising that, upon his fourth Olympic sweep, the people of Rhodes deified him. It is a commentary on the ways of glory that, of the thousands of victory statues thought to be fashioned in ancient times as likenesses of Olympic heroes, not one dependable likeness of Leonidas survives. In fact, Myron's famous, but nameless, discus thrower of the mid-fifth

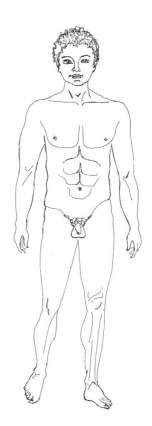

Artist's concept of Leonidas of Rhodes, whose sweep of four Olympiads establishes him as probably the greatest of ancient Olympians.

century B.C. (see this book's cover for a copy of the lost original) is one of relatively few life-size victory statues of Games champions to come down to us. Myron's athlete was probably an Olympic victor.

"There were splendid festivals," wrote Victor Duruy, "brilliant successes, unforgettable spectacles, and at other times vulgarities, disorders, ill-arranged ceremonies, and disunited processions." Duruy, a friend of Coubertin, was describing the ancient Games. However, as we will see in following chapters, he might as easily have been describing the much altered, but still recognizable, children of those Games, the Modern Olympics.

THE SUMMER GAMES

. . . there are no gains without pains.
Adlai Stevenson

Win or lose, the end of any race
is bittersweet.
Roland Huntsford

Chapter 3

STRUTTINGS AND MEANDERINGS, 1896-1936

During the first 40 years of the Modern Olympics, the Games belonged almost exclusively to Europe and America. Seven European cities and two American cities hosted the nine Summer Games of the period. The dominance is easily gauged in the heart of the Games during this era, men's track-and-field events. The early Modern Olympics saw the occasional Canadian, Australian or South African athlete win championships in these events. Even the names of two Japanese triple jumpers appeared on the victory rolls. But Europe and especially the United States clearly dominated.

Another aspect of the early Summer Games was their progress from being largely attached to various expositions to becoming festivals of real stature in and of themselves. The Games of 1900, 1904 and 1908 were held in connection with international fairs or expositions. The Stockholm Games in 1912 reversed this trend and set the Modern Olympics on course toward later recognition as the world's largest and most prestigious international festival. Women's track-and-field events were introduced in the Amsterdam Games in 1928. By the time of the Los Angeles Games in 1932, most of the events, housing arrangements, and procedures which we see today were generally in place. For example, at Los Angeles the victory and prize-giving ceremonies were combined for the first time.

The Summer Games of this period were not immune to disruption. The ancient Games ran uninterrupted for centuries through war, disaster and pestilence. But modern World War was something else. The sixth modern Olympiad, scheduled for Berlin in 1916, was cancelled due to the Great War.

The Games nevertheless expanded remarkably. From 1896 to 1928, the number of countries represented in the Olympics increased more than three-fold and the number of athletes competing increased almost ten-fold. New technologies were applied. The Games of 1912 featured for the first time electrical timing, accurately measuring events to the tenth of a second. Photo-finish equipment was also introduced in the Stockholm Games.

History was made by superstars and movie stars, by individuals and families. Paavo Nurmi of Finland came out of the north like an Arctic comet to become the world's first superstar in track events. Relentless in long-distance throughout the 1920s, Nurmi was called a "mechanical Frankenstein — created to annihilate time."

An American, Johnny Weissmuller, swam into fame from the Paris Games in 1924. Weissmuller suffered weakness as an infant and was thought to have heart problems. He developed though to become the first person to swim 100 meters in less than a minute. We remember him too as the most famous of all Tarzans.

A remarkable father-son team emerged from Sweden in shooting events. Oscar Swahn and his son, Alfred, competed in the Olympics of 1908, 1912 and 1920. Alfred also competed in the 1924 Games. Between them, during the four Olympiads, they won six gold, four silver and five bronze medals. Fifteen Olympic medals in all, a number which certainly would have increased had the 1916 Games not been cancelled. Oscar Swahn, at 72, won his last medal (silver) in the Antwerp Games in 1920 to become the oldest-ever Olympic medalist.

The first 40 years launched and secured the modern Games as permanent institutions of world renown. It was a time of coming together and pulling apart, a time of struttings and meanderings.

ATHENS, 1896

According to the official report, the opening of the first Modern Olympics in Athens "was gripping and the spectacle, indescribable." Maybe. Certainly there were enough princes and princesses on hand to populate a Disney fantasy. But the inaugural modern Games were greeted in America with something between a yawn and complete indifference. Harvard refused to excuse one of its students from class attendance in order that he might compete in the Olympics. The student, James Connolly, quit school, went to Athens, and on the first day of competition became the first Olympic champion in more than 1500 years.

The inaugural Games were hardly mentioned in the American press. The *New York Times*, for example, was

James Connolly quit school, went to Athens, and on the first day of competition became the first Olympic champion in more than 1500 years.

decidedly more interested in bicycle news than the Olympics. At the end of the first week of Olympic competition, the April 12th *Times* offered almost nothing on the Games but ran two pages on Gossip of the Cyclers and Doings of Cycle Clubs. Bicycles, the Mechanical Wonders of the World, were not only in vogue, they were the rage.

The bicycle craze hit Europe and America in the late 19th century. More than a million were in use in the United States by the end of the century. Bicycles were pushed by and for everyone, including women. "Cycling," according to one magazine in 1896, "builds up their feeble frames" and cheers "their dull and sordid thoughts".

In terms of outside contemporary interest, therefore, the most heralded victors of the Athens Games may have been the cycling cham-

The French cycling team with Paul Masson at left. To an indifferent outside world, he may have been the most heralded victor of the Athens Games.

pions. The French sent only two cyclists but they were the class of the Games. Paul Masson of France won three first places.

But unquestionably the champion most heralded locally in Athens was a Greek, Spiridon Loues, winner of the Marathon race. The event was a completely new sport and was laid out to approximate the course of the runner Pheidippides, who brought to Athens the news of the signal victory at Marathon. The race in 1896 was over a distance of 40,000 meters, just under 25 miles. It is estimated that the total crowd which viewed the event, perhaps 120,000 people, was the largest for a peaceful celebration in the history of the modern world up to that time.* The whole population of Athens at the time was slightly less than 120,000.

Loues, a shepherd from the hills near Athens, was among a field of 25 at the outset. At the halfway point, he was behind by 3000 meters. He stopped briefly for a glass of wine. Greeks took over strongly in the first three places, Loues being the leader after the 33-kilometer mark. He ran now accompanied by "an honor guard" of peasants from his village.

When Loues entered the Olympic stadium, the huge crowd exploded. The slight runner was joined by the 6' 5" Prince George of Greece, who ran alongside in full uniform to the finish. Even the normally staid *London Times* reported that "the scene baffles description."

Loues, a national hero, was showered with gifts, most of which he seems to have refused. Daily meals for ten years were offered by a hotel owner. The ancient tradition of free meals for Athenian champions in the Olympics, established under the law of Solon, had not been completely forgotten. Loues faded from Olympic view and was seen prominently only once more. The scene was tragic innocence. In the Berlin Games in 1936, the 64-year-old peasant from Maroussi, "dressed in fustanella and smiling his modest smile, carried forward a bouquet of flowers and presented them to Adolf Hitler."

More than two-thirds of the athletes in the Athens Games were Greek. Among the 13 nations represented were the United States, Britain and France, though all three teams were unofficial. The Greeks provided the Olympic organization, the site, almost all of

* *The Circus Maximus in ancient Rome seated 350,000 spectators.*

the officials, and all of the money for the Games only to see foreigners win a disproportionate share of first places. Little wonder that Loues' victory in the Marathon at the end of the Games sparked wild celebration.

There were no gold medalists as such in the Athens Games. Only first and second places in events were awarded. Winners got a silver medal, a diploma and a crown of olive branches. For second place, the athlete received a bronze medal, a diploma and a crown of laurel.

Not a single world record was set in Athens but there were notable performances by country and individual. American athletes won 9 of 12 Olympic crowns in track and field. Tom Burke won both the 100 and 400-meter races, a feat never since repeated in the modern Games. His American teammate, Robert Garrett, won the discus and shot put, and placed second in the long jump and third in the high jump. Amazingly, Garrett had never seen a real discus before arriving in Athens. The discus toss, like the Marathon race, was introduced for the first time as a modern sport in these inaugural Games.

Germany's Karl Schumann was possibly the Games' most versatile athlete. He won the open wrestling competition as well as individual and team first places in gymnastics. Not as successful, but at least as ambitious, was France's Albin Lermusiaux, who trained simultaneously for the 100 and 800-meter events and the Marathon race. When asked how, he blithely responded: "One day, I run a lettle way, vairy queek. Ze next day, I run a long way, vairy slow." He placed third in an event for which he apparently did not train, the 1500-meter race.

In the flush of victory in the triple jump, the first finals of the Modern Olympic era, James Connolly sent an excited (and immodest) telegram to his parents and friends in America: "The Greeks have conquered Europe; I have conquered the world." This estimate was vastly overstated. The world took little note of events in Athens. Only later would it decide that something indeed special had been launched there.

PARIS, 1900

Greece attempted after 1896 to keep the Games on a permanent basis. The Greek bid was supported by American Olympic athletes and others. But the crafty Coubertin spirited the Games away to his birthplace, Paris. All did not go well. The Games were a mere side show of the Universal Paris Exposition. What ensued was a collage of sports that ran in confused fashion from May to October.

Athletes outnumbered spectators at the opening ceremony in July of what was billed as the World's Amateur Track and Field Championships. Americans won 17 of 23 events. Alvin Kraenzlein of the University of Pennsylvania won four gold medals. He revolutionized hurdling by clearing the barriers with one leg extended. One of the problems at Paris, though, was that bushes grew under some of the hurdles.

Women (11 of them) participated as Olympians for the first time in history at Paris. Charlotte Cooper became the first female gold medalist by winning lawn tennis championships in women's singles and mixed doubles.

An unnamed French boy coxed the winning Netherlands pair in rowing to become the youngest gold medalist of all time. A French bakery boy won the Marathon. But the high point of the Games for the French came with their 25 to 16 victory over Germany in the exhibition rugby finals. For the first time in 30 years, combatant Frenchmen had prevailed over their long-time antagonists on a field of strife. Sedan was partially avenged. All of Paris celebrated.

Coubertin did not. Looking back on the poorly organized and unmanicured Paris Games, he admitted that "We have made a hash of our work."

ST. LOUIS, 1904

Things did not go much better in St. Louis, where the Olympics were held in connection with the 1904 World's Fair. The Games had been scheduled for Chicago, but when conflicts arose, the site was changed to St. Louis in a deal arbitrated by the country's new and sports-minded president, Theodore Roosevelt.

These international Games, if they can be called that, were owned, operated and monopolized by Americans, who won 21 of 22 events in track and field. An 18-year-old American, James Lightbody, did heavy work in winning three gold medals, one of which represented a world record in the 1500-meter race. The Games produced the first black Olympic medalist, America's George Poage, who took the bronze in the 200-meter hurdles.

Not many foreign athletes made the trip to distant St. Louis. Only 92 foreigners, 41 from neighboring Canada, were among the 687 athletes who competed in the Games. Britain sent a single athlete, Thomas Kiely, who was actually an Irishman. But he won the "all-rounder" championship, forerunner of the decathlon. Its one-day program, in succession, consisted of: the 100-yard dash, shot put, high jump, 880-yard walk, hammer throw, pole vault, 120-yard hurdles, 56-pound weight toss, long jump, and the mile run.

The first known case of a drug-assisted Olympic victory occurred in St. Louis. Unless we count Loues' glass of wine eight years prior. America's Thomas Hicks, fortified with cognac and strychnine, won the Marathon. The use of sulfate of strychnine in small amounts was fairly common among early long-distance runners. The drugs evidently were not of much help to Hicks, whose time of about three and a half hours was the slowest for the Marathon in Olympic history.

The Games were off course on fairgrounds and poorly attended. An associate of Coubertin referred to the St. Louis Olympics essentially as a freak show: "I was not only present at a sporting contest but also at a fair where there were sports, where there was cheating, where monsters were exhibited for a joke."

But the St. Louis Games did not pass without at least some comfort. Those in August attendance there were able to enjoy, at the 1904 World's Fair, two culinary innovations, the ice cream *cone* and something called the "hot dachshund sausage". The latter soon came to be known as the *hot dog*.

LONDON, 1908

After the lame spectacles of 1900 and 1904, Greece again tried, without success, to establish itself as the permanent home of the

Modern Olympics. The Intercalated Games, or Interim Games as they are sometimes called, were held in Athens in 1906. However, they are not recognized as official Games.

The Olympic mire continued in 1908 with the London Games, where July downpours were daily fare. Lawn tennis, for example, had to be moved to indoor courts.

King Edward VII, with Queen Alexandra at his side, opened the Games. Edward is remembered for his appetite both for food married with wine and for attractive women married to someone else. He is the monarch whose picture later adorned a cigar box. He is the monarch about whom it was slyly said that "greater love hath no man than this, that a man lay down his wife for his king."

The Games were launched amid political rumbling. The Finns, ruled by Russia, received the czar's permission to compete as a team but were denied permission to march under the flag of Finland. Refusing to march under the Russian banner, the Finns decided to go flagless. They may have been somewhat consoled when they left London with five Olympic medals while Russia won only one.

Protests marred the London Games. All events were judged by British officials, whose rulings were protested frequently by the Irish, Swedes, Finns, Italians, and chiefly the Americans. The uproar was so great that the International Olympic Committee afterward turned over the control and judging of individual Olympic competitions to the international federation governing each sport.

Nevertheless, the 1908 Games produced the most impressive Olympic performances seen to that time. Seven world records were broken in track and field, while four were broken in swimming. Top individual performances in track and field belonged to two Americans.

Ray Ewry of the U.S. team won his tenth and final Olympic gold medals in the 1908 Games. In three Olympiads from 1900 through 1908, and in the Intercalated Games of 1906, Ewry showed himself to be the greatest athlete of all time in standing jump events. He owned the standing high jump, long jump and triple jump competitions. Although they were soon discontinued as Olympic

Ray Ewry won ten gold medals from 1900 through 1908 but the Intercalated Games of 1906 are not officially recognized.

events, Ewry remains the only athlete ever to accumulate double-digit first places in Modern Olympic competition.

America's "Peerless Mel" Sheppard was the first in a long line of journalist-named stars. Inspired in ink or otherwise. He won the 800 and 1500-meter races in London, setting new world and Olympic records respectively. In less than two decades, Mel would be commonplace and then forgotten by the press with the rise of "Peerless Paavo" Nurmi.

The most popular Olympian of the Games was an Italian, Dorando Pietri, in the Marathon. He was small and short-legged, but he deflected questions about his legs by quoting Abraham Lincoln. Pietri insisted that his legs, like those of the ideal soldier alluded to by Lincoln, were "exactly long enough to reach from the hips to the ground".

The Princess of Wales wanted to provide a special summer treat for the royal grandchildren, their own 75 long-distance runners for a few minutes in the afternoon. Thus, the Marathon was started by the princess herself from the wide lawns of Windsor Castle, located 26 miles and 385 yards from the stadium, the now-traditional distance for the race.

Charles Hefferon of South Africa led for much of the way into London, but first into the stadium was Pietri, the candy maker from Capri, drained of body sugar and energy. The exhausted Italian, running a minute ahead of America's Johnny Hayes, turned in the wrong direction and then staggered and collapsed on the track. British officials helped him to stand up, pointed him in the right direction, and assisted him to the finish line. The intervention predictably was protested. Pietri was disqualified and the race was awarded to Hayes, the youngest member of the U.S. Olympic team.

But Pietri had won the sympathy and hearts of the British. Queen Alexandra later presented him with a huge gold cup.

The British could afford to be magnanimous. They had scored heavily in boxing, cycling, shooting and tennis. Great Britain won more Olympic gold medals (56) in London than won by all of the other 21 countries combined.

STOCKHOLM, 1912

The Modern Olympics got back on track in July 1912 with the Stockholm Games. They were well organized, officiated and reported. For the first time, the Games were "front page stuff". They featured a glimpse and an insight, many successes and some might-have-beens.

Glimpsed fleetingly was a young man destined for fame outside the realm of sport. Lieutenant George Smith Patton, the "Blood and Guts" Patton of World War II, placed fifth in a new sport, the modern pentathlon. Many years later, he sounded apologetic about his lack of success: "I don't know whether I lost my nerve or my ammunition was defective, but I did nothing like my best."

Insight into the Games as politics was possible for the first time in clear dimension at Stockholm. Russia did not recognize the autonomy of Finland and now protested the Finnish presence. Austria protested Bohemia's presence for similar reason. As will be seen, political confrontation has since become common in the Games, despite the unequivocal language of the Olympic Rules' Article 46, which states, "The Olympic Games are not competitions between nations."

But the Stockholm Games also featured for the first time Olympians from all five continents competing together, the first Olympic competition for women swimmers, and the first fine arts competition on a Modern Olympic program. Prizes in the latter were given in architecture, literature, music, painting and sculpture. As discussed in Chapter 1, Coubertin won the award in literature, the only Olympic prize ever received by the father of the modern Games. The arts contests were discontinued after 1948, but were replaced by the Cultural Olympics outside the official Olympic program.

The 1912 Games contained titanic struggles and brilliant successes. One wrestling contest in the Greco-Roman style (use of the legs for attack or defense is not permitted) lasted 11 hours. Another match, the championship in the light heavyweight division, ended in a draw after nine hours. No gold medal was awarded. Instead, the two contestants, Anders Ahlgren of Sweden and Ivar Bohling of Finland, each received a silver medal.

Eight world records were broken at Stockholm. The first in this century's long line of American superstar swimmers appeared in the person of Duke Kahanamoku, a young Hawaiian. The first of the famous Flying Finns, Hannes Kolehmainen, ruled in middle and long-distance track events. One of the greatest athletes of the century, Jim Thorpe, was a member of the U.S. track and field team. The crowns of victory and the shadows of what might have been are found in the wake of each of these three extraordinary athletes.

Kahanamoku won the 100-meter swim at Stockholm and repeated this victory in the 1920 Games with a world-record time. He certainly would have been favored to win also in 1916 had those Games not been cancelled. Thus, Kahanamoku might have become the only male swimmer in Modern Olympic history to win three times in the 100-meter event.

"Hannes the Mighty" Kolehmainen won three individual gold medals and one team silver medal in distance races in 1912. His victory by just one second in the 5000-meter race was the most dramatic of the Games. He returned, at 31, in the 1920 Games to win the Marathon with an Olympic record. Had the 1916 Games been held, Kolehmainen, at his peak, almost certainly would have won several more Olympic crowns, perhaps enough to have rivaled the record nine gold medals of the Flying Finn who followed him, Paavo Nurmi.

The shadow of circumstance applied most darkly, however, to the most popular athlete of the 1912 Games, Jim Thorpe. This twice All-American football halfback achieved what was never managed afterward. He won both the track-and-field pentathlon and the decathlon. The former consisted of the long jump, javelin, discus, and the 200 and 1500-meter races. It was discontinued after 1924. The decathlon consisted of all of the foregoing events except the 200-meter race, and included as well six more events: the high jump, pole vault, shot put, 110-meter hurdles, and the

Jim Thorpe was voted the greatest all-around athlete of the first half of the 20th century.

100 and 400-meter races. Thorpe, an American Indian, won the pentathlon and decathlon by wide margins. At the close of the Games, Sweden's King Gustav said to him, "Sir, you are the most wonderful athlete in the world." Thorpe claimed that two words filled his response: "Thanks, King."

When Thorpe died in 1953, he was buried in Mauch Chunk. The town gave up little in agreeing to change its name, in exchange for the mortal remains of the athlete, to Jim Thorpe, Pennsylvania.

But Thorpe's achievement was denied him in life. He was stripped of his Olympic medals after it was learned in 1913 that he had played semiprofessional baseball one summer for $60 a month. In a 1950 poll of American sportswriters by the Associated Press, Thorpe was voted to be the greatest male athlete of the first half of the 20th century. Efforts to reinstate his Olympic crowns were blocked for many years, but in 1982 the International

Olympic Committee relinquished and Thorpe's name was returned to the record book. When Thorpe died in 1953, he was buried in Mauch Chunk. The town gave up little in agreeing to change its name, in exchange for the mortal remains of the athlete, to Jim Thorpe, Pennsylvania.

It is well that the Stockholm Games rekindled the Olympic flame in bright fashion. The winds of war were about to extinguish many of the lights of Europe. The Games were merely one of whole ranks of civilized institutions to be sorely tested. Had the 1912 Games been less than a resounding success, the Modern Olympics may not have survived the catastrophic interval that followed.

BERLIN, 1916

The VI Modern Olympiad was not held. The big event in 1916 was at the Somme, and whatever semblance of glory to be had would be sought not in the stadium but in the trenches. The Olympic crown was eclipsed by the steel helmet. The Olympic medal was replaced by a cross, whether Iron, Victoria, or plain white in Flanders.

ANTWERP, 1920

The Modern Olympics resumed in August 1920 with hastily organized Games in still-devastated Belgium. Antwerp's selection as host city was not without meaning. No country had suffered more than Belgium in the Great War. The defeated nations of Germany, Austria and Hungary were not invited. Victors often not only write the history but literally decide the rules of the game in other ways as well.

The Olympic flag flew for the first time. The symbol of the Games, the five rings appearing on the flag, was taken from an emblem discovered in the ruins of Olympia by Coubertin in 1913. Victor Boin, a Belgian fencer, took the first Olympic oath at the opening ceremony on behalf of the 2600 competitors. Some 2000 white pigeons were released for the first time as part of the ceremony.

Notwithstanding the aftermath of war, the Olympics were held on the largest scale to that time. They were thinly attended but the Games were taking on the rituals which are clearly recognizable today.

The outstanding athlete of the 1920 Games was to be the Olympic athlete of the decade, Paavo Nurmi. The 23-year-old Nurmi won three gold medals at Antwerp and launched a track career unexcelled in modern sport. During the 1920s, this greatest of the Flying Finns set world records at every distance from 1500 to 20,000 meters. Nurmi ironically began his stellar Olympic career with a loss, being surprised at the end of the 5000-meter race by the sudden burst of a French runner. But Peerless Paavo would seldom be overtaken again in his remarkable stretch of victories.

During the three Olympiads from 1920 through 1928, Nurmi ran in ten individual distance events. After taking the silver medal in his first Olympic race, Nurmi then won seven individual gold medals in a row, followed by two silver medals. He won two gold medals in team events during these years. He trained as a youth by racing against the

Paavo Nurmi of Finland was called a "mechanical Frankenstein — created to annihilate time."

local mail train in Finland. He ran in maturity with the relentlessness of a locomotive.

The Finnish team tied with the United States in the number of gold medals won in track-and-field events in the Antwerp Games. Each had nine. Little Finland, a country of only three million people, had equaled the performances of athletes from a nation of 106 million people.

The first man to be popularly labeled the World's Fastest Human was Charles Paddock of the U.S. track team. He won the

100-meter sprint and led the way in the 400-meter relay victory. Another track medalist was destined for a Nobel prize. Philip Noel-Baker, silver medalist for Britain in the 1500-meter race, would receive the Nobel Memorial Prize in Peace in 1959. Noel-Baker was a life-long pacifist and worked tirelessly for both the League of Nations and the United Nations. One of his stated views was reminiscent of Coubertin: "In the nuclear age, sport is man's best hope."

Italy's best hope in Antwerp was a fencer, Nedo Nadi, called by some the greatest and most versatile fencer of the century. Nadi won individual and team first places in foil and saber and a team gold medal in epee. He was the first Olympian ever to win five gold medals in a single Games. He added these to an Olympic crown in individual foil won in Stockholm. Nadi later was president of the Italian Fencing Federation.

Britain's Albert Hill, a 36-year-old railway guard, won the 800 and 1500-meter events in Antwerp, and developed an interesting training technique in the process. While others fought pre-race jitters, he took an early lunch and then a three-hour nap prior to each race.

Jack Kelly, a formidable individual oarsman, won the single and double sculls events. A bricklayer from Philadelphia, Kelly by historic stroke was also father of Princess Grace of Monaco.

Just over one-third the age of Hill, an American child-Olympian, Aileen Riggen, at 13 won the springboard diving championship, the youngest person to that date to take an individual Olympic crown. Exactly twice the age of Hill, a Swedish marksman, Oscar Swahn, at 72 won a silver medal, the oldest-ever Olympic medalist.

The Antwerp Games had some interesting ripples. The U.S. Olympic Team traveled to Europe aboard a cramped and aged transport ship. It had been used as a funeral ship during the war and still reeked of formaldehyde. The Americans won the eight-oared rowing competition in Antwerp, and thus began one of the fabled dynasties of the Modern Olympics, 40 years of championships which ended when the Germans won the competition in the 1960 Games. Jack Kelly, a formidable individual oarsman, won

the single and double sculls events. A bricklayer from Philadelphia, Kelly by historic stroke was also father of Princess Grace
of Monaco.

Although the United States did not dominate track and field in
the 1920 Games, as in previous Olympics, it still accumulated 41
gold medals in all sports, more than twice as many championships
as the runner-up in the unofficial standings, Sweden with 19.

PARIS, 1924

In July 1924, Paris became the first city to repeat as host of the
modern Summer Games. Coubertin wanted to get it right this
time. The first Winter Games had been held earlier in the year,
also in France, at Chamonix.

The Olympic motto made its first appearance in the Paris
Games. The phrase *Citius, Altius, Fortius* ("Swifter, Higher,
Stronger") was coined in 1921 by a French cleric, Pere Henri
Didon. The Games in fact did soar above the sad spectacle of the
second Olympiad in turn-of-the-century Paris. But the 44 nations
participating did not include Germany, which was excluded by the
French on the pretext that the safety of German athletes could
not be assured.

The United States won 45 gold medals, more first places than
the next four nations of France, Finland, Britain and Italy combined. Americans dominated swimming as they had in 1920, winning more gold medals (13) in these events than in any other
sport.

Johnny Weissmuller was the king of the water. He won three
gold medals by way of the 100 and 400-meter freestyle events and
the 800-meter relay. He would repeat as victor at 100 meters in
1928, the last male swimmer to score successive Olympic triumphs for this distance.

Part of Weissmuller's success was due to a relaxed style. "I did-
n't tense up," he explained. That was in the water. His movie
career hardly evoked the Royal Shakespeare Company. But a stiff
demeanor as an actor did not for a moment stop his big splash as
the most famous of Hollywood's Tarzans.

Also on the waters in Paris was the young Benjamin Spock, who was to gain fame as a baby doctor. He rowed to the eight-oared victory with the Yale crew.

Britain scored its greatest triumphs in Paris with track victories at 100, 400 and 800 meters, much of the drama of which was captured in the 1981 film *Chariots of Fire*. At least one celluloid fact though needs amendment. The British sprinter who was the hero of the movie, Harold Abrahams, was hardly the driven athlete in training as depicted on the screen. He frequently took his glass of ale and enjoyed cigars as well, habits which horrified the U.S. track coaches.

The sun was rising for black Olympians. America's DeHart Hubbard and Ned Gourdin finished first and second respectively in the long jump, thus becoming the first Afro-Americans to win gold and silver Olympic medals. The luster of Hubbard's victory was only diminished slightly by the fact that fellow American Robert LeGendre registered the longest jump of the Games, setting a new world record, while competing in the pentathlon.

The world was introduced to the quality of South American soccer when Uruguay cruised to the championship, beating the Swiss 3-0 in the finals before a packed crowd in Colombe stadium. Soccer traditionally draws the greatest number of spectators among those attending Olympic events. Uruguay repeated as Olympic champions in 1928, defeating Argentina. Although South America has produced some of the world's best soccer teams and players, Uruguay remains to date the only non-European country ever to win an Olympic crown in soccer.

But the preeminent Olympic star was again Paavo Nurmi. He won five gold medals in the Paris Games. His highest achievement was a double victory, at 1500 and 5000 meters, inside the space of little more than one incredible hour. With some justification, Grantland Rice called Nurmi a "superman".

What made Nurmi tick? Simplistic notions were cooked up in the press about austere diet and the toughening effects of the sauna. Nurmi was said to live on black bread and dried fish. His favorite food actually seems to have been oatmeal. Beyond challenge by other runners, Nurmi ran against the clock as if possessed. He carried a stopwatch while running and referred to it with cold and unsettling concentration.

Nurmi apparently ate neither bread nor fish nor oatmeal so much as he ate the lunch of other runners.

AMSTERDAM, 1928

The 1928 Games, held between May and August, would be the last Modern Olympics to meander for months across the calendar. Subsequent modern Summer Games would be programmed for 16 days.

The Modern Olympics reached full glow in Amsterdam. An Olympic flame for the first time was lighted in a tower of the stadium and burned throughout the Games. The Olympics achieved for the first time the broad representation and sharing of honors which are central to the spirit of the Games. Some 46 participating nations were represented by over 3000 athletes, 290 of whom were women (more than four times the number of women participating in Antwerp). Gold medals were won by 28 countries. It would be 40 years, in the Mexico City Games, before more countries would find success in the Olympic gold rush.

Track-and-field events for women made their Olympic debut. Women competed in the 100 and 800-meter races, 400-meter relay, discus and high jump. A controversy arose because of the physical toll on runners in the 800-meter event. A longer Olympic distance for women runners would not be seen for 44 years, when the 1500-meter event was added in the Munich Games.

The United States maintained its winning ways but not without challenge. Germany, competing in the Olympics for the first time in 16 years, made a strong showing across the board, winning water polo and riding high in equestrian events. Germans traditionally have been among the leaders in Olympic events on horseback. Germany's total of 10 gold medals in Amsterdam was second only to the 22 won by the United States.

The Finns remained big favorites, especially in the Olympic centerpiece of track and field. They won five gold medals in these events. Nurmi won at 10,000 meters and ran second to Finnish winners in the 3000-meter steeplechase and 5000-meter race, thus bringing his final count to nine gold and three silver medals in three Olympiads. Many thought that Nurmi may have held back in order to spread the Olympic gold among his countrymen.

Such generosity, though, would have been out of character for Nurmi. After his narrow victory over a countryman at 10,000 meters, a reporter observed that "Nurmi demonstrated that he's the same aloof figure by refusing to shake Ritola's hand and unceremoniously waving aside cameramen as he trotted off the field."

Nurmi was also one of the most outstanding examples of the Finnish concept of *sisu*. This word, actually more like a creed, means both physical and mental toughness. It stands for endurance and will power. *Sisu* might be loosely translated as "you can't beat me." No other concept projects better than does *sisu* the national spirit of Finland and especially its athletes of this period. Nurmi seemed driven by the *sisu* creed. That he would hold back in an Olympic competition is not easily believed.

Swift-of-foot Davy Burghley, later Lord Exeter, would undergo two hip-replacement operations. After the second operation in 1971, he had the first artificial hip plated in silver and mounted on the hood of his Rolls-Royce as a mascot.

Other highlights in Amsterdam included India's victory over Holland in field hockey. The match was seen by 50,000 spectators and was the beginning of India's 32-year reign in the sport.

Britain's Lord David Burghley, a nobleman who answered to "Davy", won the 400-meter low hurdles. He was one of the most popular figures of all time within the Olympic establishment and became a vice-president of the International Olympic Committee. Swift-of-foot Davy Burghley, later Lord Exeter, would undergo two hip-replacement operations. After the second operation in 1971, he had the first artificial hip plated in silver and mounted on the hood of his Rolls-Royce as a mascot.

The Far East saw its first gold medalists in Japan's Mikio Oda, winner of the triple jump, and Yoshiyuki Tsuruta, who won the 200-meter breaststroke in swimming. Japan repeated its victories in the triple jump in 1932 and 1936. And Tsuruta in 1932 successfully defended his Olympic crown in the 200-meter breaststroke, the only repeat winner ever in this event.

General Douglas MacArthur, a man to encounter the Japanese, wrote in his official report on the 1928 Games that "Nothing is more synonymous of our national success than is our national success in athletics." But as Robert Graves and his generation had learned in the trenches in the prior decade, words are never more suspect than when committed to an official report.

LOS ANGELES, 1932

With much of the world in financial collapse, the Games which began on July 30, 1932, might have been called the depression Olympics. But there was nothing threadbare about them. The Coliseum, a magnificent stadium for 105,000 spectators, contained a "springboard track" of crushed peat which most runners agreed was the best they had ever seen. A specially constructed Olympic Village was introduced for the 1300 men athletes. The Games' 127 women athletes were housed in a posh Los Angeles hotel.

The Olympic Village kitchens daily processed tons of food: 1800 pounds of fresh peas, 2750 pounds of string beans, 50 huge bags of potatoes, 450 gallons of ice cream, and untold loads of bread, meat and beverages. All of this was done at a cost of less than two dollars a day for each athlete.

Victory stands were used for the first time. On them winners received their Olympic medals accompanied by the playing of the national anthems and the raising of the flags of the winners' countries. An electric photo-finish device was introduced to determine races questionable to the human eye. The equipment got early use in confirming the razor-thin results in the 100-meter dash.

The 1932 Games were the most financially successful to that time and ended with a surplus of about a million dollars. The Los Angeles Games of 1984 would also be an impressive financial success, something which is hardly a given in the staging of the Modern Olympics. The 1932 Games owed their black ink chiefly to ticket sales to well over a million spectators.

Among the spectators were Jim Thorpe and Paavo Nurmi. Thorpe, an alcoholic at 44 and down on his luck, showed up at the Los Angeles Games without the price of admission. His ticket was bought by an old fan who recognized him.

Nurmi had planned to run for Finland in the Marathon and would have been favored to win. However, charges of professionalism surfaced. Nurmi was accused of receiving excessive travel expenses during a competition in Germany. "Nurmi," as one track official put it, "had the lowest heart beat and the highest asking price of any athlete in the world." These words have a strange ring today considering that modern Olympians have long since passed through the portals of the big bucks. But in 1932 it was not so, or if it was so it was not tolerated when discovered.

In any event, the Los Angeles Games opened with the neglect of giants: two of the century's greatest sports legends assigned to the peanut gallery, one because he had no money and the other because he allegedly spent money for expenses not due him.

The United States won 41 gold medals in the 1932 Summer Games, more than three times as many as second-place Italy with 12. The athletes journeying to distant Los Angeles were decidedly fewer in number than in the prior Olympiad but the quality of talent was superb. Some 19 world records and 31 Olympic records were broken.

Japan's Olympic star was on the rise. The Japanese were supreme in men's swimming in Los Angeles. They had placed 16th in the overall medals count in Amsterdam but climbed to seventh place in Los Angeles. The Finns though were beginning to fade. They were challenged by predictable contenders and by unpredictable circumstance. The latter was seen in the example of Volmari Iso-Hollo, winner of the 3000-meter steeplechase. And then some. Iso-Hollo ran an extra lap because of a mistake by the official lap counter. The Finn's victory is the only one entombed in the record book with mistake attached.

America's black athletes were beginning to win Olympic crowns in numbers. Eddie Tolan won both the 100 and 200-meter sprints. His was a photo-finish at 100 meters. He was two inches ahead of Ralph Metcalfe. Edward Gordon won the broad jump.

The top woman athlete in the Games was an American, Mildred "Babe" Didrikson. Shortly before the Olympics, *she* won the U.S.

women's track-and-field championship. Which is to say that she, as a one-woman team from Texas, entered eight events in the 1932 women's national championship, winning five and tying for first place in a sixth event. In distant second place overall was a team of 22 women athletes from Illinois.

Women were allowed to enter only three events in the early modern Games.

"Babe" Didrikson said that she played everything but dolls.

Organizers believed that women's body structure dictated that they not be physically overtaxed. At Los Angeles, the 18-year-old called "Babe" won the 80-meter hurdles and javelin throw but had to settle for second place officially in the high jump because of a technicality. One judge challenged her jumping technique. Her Olympic medal for the high jump was gold on one side and silver on the other, the only one of its type ever awarded to an Olympian. We can only guess what her Olympic trophy case might have looked like had she been able to enter more than three events.

After the Olympics, Didrikson went on to become an All-American basketball player for three years. Turning to golf, she won 17 international titles before early death from cancer at 42. Someone once asked if there was anything she did not play. "Yeah," she replied. "Dolls." In the same poll of American sportswriters that honored Jim Thorpe, "Babe" Didrikson Zaharias in 1950 was named as the greatest woman athlete of the first half of the 20th century.

The 1932 Games saw a mingling of success and tragedy in the story of William Carr, the young American winner in what is remembered as one of the greatest 400-meter finals in Modern Olympic history. Trailing into the stretch, Carr went to fluid overdrive and shredded the world record. The runner-up also broke the world record. Carr, a junior at Penn, looked down a road promising long athletic brilliance. But there was a tragic intersection. Eight months after the Los Angeles Games, an auto accident left Bill Carr with both legs broken, never again to run competitively.

The modern Games were to pass now from the City of the Angels to Germany. For the first time since the rule of the Romans, the Olympics would open under the blessing and eye of a dictator.

Chapter 4

BIG SHOW, BIG GAP AND BIG CHILL, 1936-1956

The two decades following 1936 were the most tumultuous of the century. Changes in the Modern Olympics nearly matched those elsewhere in the international sphere. The Berlin Games of 1936 outstripped all preceding Olympics in scale and grandeur. The Olympics survived the trauma of world war and produced two postwar Games which exceeded even those of Berlin in sheer size.

Some 4.5 million tickets were purchased during the Berlin Games, three times the number sold for the Los Angeles Games. The Olympics were televised for the first time in Berlin, with 160,000 viewers watching on a closed-circuit system. Over 4900 athletes competed in the 1952 Olympics in Helsinki, three times the number in Los Angeles and almost 2000 more athletes than had competed in Amsterdam. The Games in Berlin and afterward literally assumed Olympian proportions.

Hitler spent $30 million to make the 1936 Games a showcase. He succeeded. The Berlin Olympics were organized with Germanic precision. Although glazed with politics and propaganda, they were brilliantly orchestrated. They proved a mixed blessing. It was said that they "were grandoise and oppressing" and "caused bitter resentment but widened the awareness of the Olympic Movement." The 1936 Games were probably the most celebrated and spectacular festival the world had seen in 1800 years, since the time of Hadrian in Rome.

However, the Big Show in Berlin in no way insulated the Olympics, and certainly not mankind, from the precipice of the Second World War. The Olympics may be paved with good intentions but they represent no special detour for those bent on plunging the way to hell. The international celebration of sport failed to prevent the carnage at Stalingrad, just as it failed to prevent that at Verdun almost 30 years prior and just as it has failed to prevent the savaging of today's Sarajevo.

If Hitler had prevailed, the Modern Olympics well may have continued but the choreography would have been that of Wagner or Speer rather than Coubertin. Fate though saw the 1948 Olympics in London, where the British national anthem by design was played only twice, at the opening and closing ceremonies. That was 478 fewer times than the German anthem was heard at the Berlin Games. The 1948 Olympics were the first real postwar opportunity to apply balm, or at least rouge, to an international face disfigured by events in battle and concentration camps.

The three Olympiads of this period ran from the sublime, through tragedy and into the banal. The Nazis snubbed America's black athletes but that did not chill human excellence. Jesse Owens won four gold medals. "Theories of a master race collided with a fact: a master racer." Nonetheless, a war followed which extinguished untold lives and hopes and which nearly extinguished the Olympic flame as we know it.

Out of these times of glacial events and grief came the banal tags of sportswriters. They advertised Jesse Owens as the Tan Streak or, less stimulating, the Cafe-au-Lait Cyclone. The great track star of the 1948 and 1952 Games, Emil Zatopek, was dubbed the Mad Czech and Emil the Terrible. His specialties, the 5,000 and 10,000-meter races, became "the Woolworth double". Fanny Blankers-Koen, the Dutch woman who electrified the track world in the 1948 Games, was referred to as the Flying Housewife or, worse, Marvelous Mama. Bob Richards, an American clergyman and the pole vault champion in the 1952 and 1956 Games, was tagged all too predictably as the Vaulting Vicar.

Through the litter of war and sprained nicknames, however, a pattern of sorts emerges for the Olympics during this period. It is an unfortunate one. The Berlin Olympics were staged to impress the world at large but also to draw an imposing line of division between the so-called master race and visitors to *their* Games. But an equally blatant division surfaced 16 years later in

Helsinki, where two Olympic Villages had to be constructed, one for Eastern bloc athletes and one for the rest. It was as if nothing had been learned through the vast struggles and disasters. The world, and the Olympic vessel within it, seemingly moved during these two decades from divisiveness, through war and into a divisiveness of different paint but wider stripe. This drift clearly was not what promoters had in mind when they spoke glibly of an Olympic Movement.

The world, and the Olympic vessel within it, moved during these two decades from divisiveness, through war and into a divisiveness of different paint but wider stripe. This drift clearly was not what promoters had in mind when they spoke glibly of an Olympic Movement.

BERLIN, 1936: "THE BRIGHT FACE OF DANGER"

Robert Lewis Stevenson somewhere refers to "The bright face of danger." Seldom has that brightness shown more intensely than in the Berlin Games that opened on the first day of August in 1936.

Germany's Gotthard Handrick takes aim.

The contours of danger were observable in the chiseled Teutonic figure and imperial war chariot on the Games' official poster. The danger was readily observable again in the look, demeanor and equipment of the Games' modern pentathlon champion as seen at left. In this bright and concentrated Aryan face, there is more than a hint of ruthlessness.

The face of 1936 was not the one originally intended by Olympic planners. Hitler had not come to power when Berlin was selected in 1931 to host the 1936 Summer Olympics. The Games had been awarded to the Weimar Republic not the Third Reich. It did not take long, though, for Nazi methods to be known and abhorred. Signs cropped up in Germany with venomous messages such as "Dogs and Jews are not allowed." Hitler in 1935 proclaimed the infamous "Nuremberg laws" which declared Jews to be "sub-humans".

Many in America voiced strong objections to participation in the Berlin Games. But Avery Brundage, president of the U.S. Olympic Committee, accused the protesters of "betraying the athletes of the United States." The Nazis took down the signs (temporarily) and promised no open discrimination against Jews and blacks. The Berlin Games were on.

For the first time, the Olympic flame was carried by torch from ancient Olympia to the host city. A stream of over 3000 runners, each running one kilometer (somewhat more than a half mile), brought the flame to the Olympic stadium in Berlin with its 110,000 spectators.

An early victor in the Berlin Games was Hans Woellke in the shot put, the first German ever to win a gold medal in track-and-field events. The Fuehrer was elated. But German joy, at least in track and field, was short-lived.

Enter Jesse Owens of Cleveland and Ohio State University. Indifferent to Nazi murmurings about "the Black auxiliaries", Owens proceeded to win gold medals in the 100 and 200-meter sprints, the 400-meter relay race and the long jump. Neither was Owens bothered that Hitler never extended personal congratulations to him as was done for German victors. "I didn't go over to shake hands with Hitler, anyway," Owens said. Yet all was not a cakewalk for him. He almost failed to qualify in the long jump. Down to his last try after fouling twice, Owens recalled asking, "Did I come 3,000 miles to make a fool of myself?"

Help for Owens came from an unexpected quarter. Lutz Long, an appropriately named broad-jump specialist on the German track-and-field team, suggested that Owens aim his takeoff well behind the foul line on the third jump. Owens followed the advice and qualified. After stiff competition from the second-place finisher, Owens won the gold medal with an Olympic record jump

Jesse Owens' single-Games performance in track and field would not be equaled for 48 years.

of almost 26 and one-half feet, a distance not bettered in the Olympics for 24 years. Finishing second to Owens was Lutz Long. The two athletes developed a friendship that was eclipsed by war and then ended by Long's death in combat in Sicily as a soldier in the German army.

Jesse Owens was declared the Athlete of the Games. His feat of four crowns in track and field in a single Games would not be matched until 1984, when Carl Lewis won the same four events as had Owens. Black Americans in the Berlin Games won a majority (13) of the total of 25 U.S. medals in track and field. Their remarkable record in these events had begun.

A Dutch athlete was the big winner among women competing in the 1936 Olympics. Hendrika Mastenbroek won three gold medals and one silver medal in swimming. She was the last woman to win Olympic crowns in both the 100 and 400-meter freestyle. Parting the waters also was 13-year-old Marjorie Gestring, the youngest person ever to win an Olympic gold medal. She won the springboard diving title for the United States.

Not youth but longevity was served in 1936 by the most successful oarsman and sculler of all time, Britain's Jack Beresford, who won a gold medal in the double sculls. The event features a light and narrow racing boat propelled by two persons, each with a pair of oars. Beresford competed with success in five consecutive Games from 1920 through 1936, winning a medal in each

Olympiad for a total of three gold and two silver medals. Only World War II prevented his appearance in a sixth Olympic Games in 1940.

One of the best lightweight Olympic wrestlers of all time made his final appearance in the 1936 Games. Kustaa Pihlajamaki of Finland won the freestyle featherweight (127 pounds) championship. He won the bantamweight (118 pounds) championship in 1924 and the silver medal as a featherweight in 1928. Not since Alfred Nobel, the inventor of dynamite, had a son of Scandinavia shown so effectively that explosives are often packed in small parcels.

Edoardo Mangiarotti of Italy won the first of his full chest of Olympic medals in fencing in the 1936 Games. In five successive Olympics, from 1936 through 1960, this best ever left-handed fencer won six gold, five silver and two bronze medals. Appearing in one more Olympiad than Mangiarotti, and winning one more gold medal in fencing, was Hungary's legendary Aladar Gerevich. His six Olympic Games (1932 through 1960) yielded seven championships. He also collected one silver medal and two bronze medals. What is staggering about the records of these two contemporaries is that they were compiled despite the interruption of World War II. The Big Gap created by the war probably prevented both fencers from being at or near the top of all-time Olympic gold medal winners. The war almost certainly prevented Mangiarotti from winning, by a comfortable margin, the greatest number of total Olympic medals in the history of the modern Games.

Basketball was played for the first time as an official Olympic sport in 1936. The United States easily won the gold medal to begin its 36-year domination in the sport, which ended in 1972 with a highly controversial loss to the Soviet Union in the Munich Games.

A fascinating story grew out of the Marathon competition. The race was fiercely contested at the end by Kitei Son for Japan and Britain's Ernie Harper. Nearing the finish, the Oriental runner became confused and made a wrong turn. Harper gave up literally a golden opportunity when he ran after his competitor and corrected his route. Japan's runner went on to win the race. The story has yet another fold. The winner was Korean not Japanese. In fact, his name was not Kitei Son but Sohn Kee-Chung. He was obligated to take a Japanese name and to run under Japan's banner because his country was under occupation. In the 1948 Games, after Korea had shed the Japanese yoke, Sohn carried his country's flag in South Korea's first Olympic appearance. Sohn, at 76, would later carry the Olympic torch into Seoul stadium to begin the 1988 Games.

Germany won 33 gold medals in Berlin, and the United States placed second in the unofficial (but carefully tallied) results with 24 gold medals. When the Olympic flame was extinguished, no one realized that only after a gap of 12 years and history's most costly war would it burn again.

HELSINKI, 1940, AND LONDON, 1944:
THE GAMES THAT NEVER WERE

The XII Olympiad was scheduled originally for Tokyo but this arrangement was cancelled after Japan invaded China in 1938. Helsinki was then designated as host city but the 1940 Games were cancelled altogether with the Soviet invasion of Finland and the advent of the Second World War in 1939. The Battle of Britain was raging in August 1940, the time once scheduled for the Summer Games.

The XIII Olympiad, by bad luck scheduled for London, was cancelled due to inclement conditions, the continuing world war.

LONDON, 1948:
JUMP-STARTING THE MODERN OLYMPICS

Four years late, the London Games opened on July 29, 1948, under the watchful eye and leadership of Lord David Burghley, the chairman of the British Olympic Committee. The Games were hastily but admirably organized. Given threadbare circumstances in postwar London, the approach was to use existing facilities to the extent possible. Therefore, Wembley stadium served as the central Olympic venue. A capacity crowd of 82,000 turned out to see the Modern Olympic Games jump-started.

The scars of war were still evident in heavily bombed London. Scars existed elsewhere as well. Upon Germany's defeat, the Soviets sent the entire German Olympic Committee to a concentration camp. So much for international understanding through sport. Ritter von Halt, a member of the International Olympic Committee, was imprisoned for five years by the Soviets. It was said by the Olympic Assembly, however, that von Halt during this period "never ceased to belong to the IOC", a subtle point of dubious consolation for von Halt. His health was broken when the Soviets finally released him.

Upon Germany's defeat, the Soviets sent the entire German Olympic Committee to a concentration camp. So much for international understanding through sport.

Not surprisingly, Germany and Japan were excluded from the 1948 Games. The Soviets were invited but sent only coaches and trainers to observe. The new state of Israel did not participate because of the Arab threat of boycott.

Surmounting it all, the opening ceremonies were applied and the Olympic engine turned over. More than 4000 athletes from 59 countries passed in review for the king and royal family. As was the case for the Olympics exactly 40 years prior in London, the weather during the Games was wet and miserable.

At no time was the weather worse than for the decathlon. The weather during the second day of competition was one of the most foul in Olympic records. The handsome young favorite, 17-year-old Bob Mathias, from Tulare, California, emerged from sitting under a blanket only to compete. Late into the night, the decathletes struggled for the mythical, but real enough, title of World's Greatest Athlete. Mathias, who ate an early breakfast and two box lunches during the day, by evening in the 13-hour ordeal was too tired to take food. An official held a flashlight on the foul line in order that he might see it in the javelin event. Only remnants of the original crowd of 70,000 stayed past midnight to see Mathias win.

Mathias broke the back of competitors with his second-day performances in the 110-meter hurdles, discus, javelin and pole vault. His lead was such at the end that he merely jogged through the 1500-meter race. Asked how he intended to celebrate such an arduous victory, Mathias did not respond that he was going to Disney World. He quipped instead, "Start shaving, I guess." Mathias would repeat as decathlon champion in the 1952 Games, a towering achievement matched only by the decathlon victories of Britain's Daley Thompson in the 1980 and 1984 Olympics.

Bob Mathias is one of only two athletes to win the Olympic decathlon twice.

Bob Mathias never lost a decathlon competition. He has stated recently, with some modesty, that he was "jack of all trades and master of none, although I'd like to consider myself the master of the decathlon." But regarding the Herculean victory under the floodlights in wet and cold Wembley stadium, Paul Helms said it best: "We sent a boy over to do a man's job and he did it far better than any man ever could."

In the London Games, for the first time in the Modern Olympics, no man won more than one track-and-field championship. The story was different in events for women. Fanny Blankers-Koen of Holland won four gold medals in cold and stinging rains during the three days of her competitions. Like "Babe" Didrikson and other women before her, Blankers-Koen was limited to entering three individual events. She entered neither the long jump nor the high jump although she held the world record in both events.

Her Olympic crowns came in the 80-meter hurdles, the 100 and 200-meter sprints, and the 400-meter relay race. No woman had ever won four gold medals in the Olympics, much less in a single Games.

Blankers-Koen took her successes in stride. After the Games, the Dutch paraded her through Amsterdam in an open coach drawn by four white horses. "All I've done is run fast," she said. "I don't quite see why people should make so much fuss about that."

Not much fuss was made in London about the medals count by country. The United States won 38 gold medals in all, far ahead of runner-up Sweden with 16. However, this would be the last Olympics in which a facade of casualness would be maintained in the accounting at the medals table. The Olympic shootouts between the Americans and Soviets were about to begin.

Britain won only three gold medals in the 1948 Summer Games, the first time that a large country hosting the Games had failed to lead the way in the medals count. Perhaps after their stalwart efforts during the war, the British felt that they had nothing to prove. The simple truth also was that they were drained in so many ways. In the 1952 Games, Britain would have to rely on a horse, Foxhunter, for its sole gold medal.

Five Olympians not yet noted must receive mention. The first four are not as well known as Mathias or Blankers-Koen but all four are legends in themselves. Paul Elvstrom of Denmark won the first of four gold medals in small-boat sailing in the 1948 Olympics. He won championships as well in the Games of 1952, 1956 and 1960. Also supreme on the water, in the same four Olympiads (1948-1960), was Sweden's Gert Fredriksson. He won two gold medals in canoeing in the 1948 Games, one in 1952, two in 1956, and one in 1960. Fredriksson also won a silver medal in 1952 and a bronze medal in 1960.

Raimondo d' Inzeo of Italy in 1948 competed in the first of his record eight Olympiads. From 1948 through 1976, d' Inzeo participated in equestrian events, winning one gold, two silver and three bronze medals. No other modern Olympian has exhibited such durability.

The greatest Olympic middleweight boxer of all time made his debut in the 1948 Games by winning the middleweight (165 pounds) championship. Laszlo Papp of Hungary went on also to win the light middleweight (156 pounds) boxing championship in the 1952 and 1956 Olympics. Not to detract from the athleticism needed for activities such as fencing or equestrian events, but it must be said that longevity as a champion in Olympic boxing or wrestling, cogently contact sports, carries with it special meaning.

Papp, at 36, won the European professional middleweight title in 1962 and later retired undefeated. It was by no means easy for Eastern bloc athletes of this period to break into the professional ranks. Papp, therefore, was inhibited from pursuing an illustrious and profitable professional career in the West. But then again, maybe he was better off without facing the likes of Jake La Motta, Sugar Ray Robinson and Dick Tiger.

The final athlete to be mentioned briefly is Emil Zatopek. He will receive fuller and deserved attention in the next section. In 1948 he won the Olympic 10,000-meter race but he is remembered here for something he said. Zatopek spoke with measured eloquence, and doubtless for the athletes of his generation, in observing that the 1948 Games were "a liberation of the human spirit — after all those dark days of the war." The abominable overcast in London ultimately produced a silver lining. The Olympics were back.

HELSINKI, 1952: EAST VERSUS WEST

Finland's living sports legend, 55-year-old Paavo Nurmi, was the final relay runner who brought the Olympic torch into Helsinki stadium to open the Games on July 19, 1952. A thunderous roar went up from the crowd. There would be little else for the Finns to celebrate. For the first time in 40 years, they did not win a single gold medal in Olympic track-and-field events.

Germany and Japan were permitted to rejoin the Olympic fold. The Russians agreed to participate only after separate living quarters were provided for Soviet bloc athletes. That meant two Olympic Villages, one each for East and West. Coubertin had not contemplated the needs of Joseph Stalin.

Although the 1948 Games were the first ever for the Soviets, their team was the largest at Helsinki, and it lost no time in flexing its muscle. Russians virtually swept gymnastics. Viktor Chukarin entered six events, winning four gold and two silver medals. A full menu of women's gymnastics was begun in Helsinki and Soviet women instantly revealed their talent. Maria Gorokhovskaya won two gold and five silver medals in gymnastics, the most medals ever won by a woman in a single Games. The Russians also showed depth in wrestling and women's track and field. Soviet women won all three places in the discus toss.

Something momentous had happened. The Olympics were to be influenced by the political contest between East and West. And the United States would not again go unchallenged as the premier Olympic power.

Not that the Americans did badly in Helsinki. They won a total of 40 gold medals as opposed to 22 for the Soviets. The United States showed especially well in men's track and field, men's swimming, and in boxing. Floyd Patterson, at age 17, won as a middleweight but had problems with language: "Every time I get my suit pressed, it costs me 300 kilocycles." Eddie Sanders, the U.S. heavyweight, won in the finals over Ingemar Johansson of Sweden. Johansson as a professional would later enjoy a short reign by defeating heavyweight champion Patterson. In Helsinki, though, Johansson spent most of the finals running for his life and was disqualified for "not trying". He received no Olympic medal.

However, the hero of the 1952 Games was neither Russian nor American. Emil Zatopek, a Czech army officer and son of a humble carpenter, proved himself the greatest distance runner since Nurmi. The Czech was the first and only Olympian ever to win the 5000 and 10,000 meter races and the Marathon in a single Games. The feat was all the more remarkable because Zatopek had never previously run a Marathon in competition. But adventure was nothing new for Zatopek. He had run the 10,000-meter race only twice prior to winning the event four years before in the London Games.

Zatopek's sense of gamesmanship was as sturdy as his legs.

During the 1952 Marathon, he allowed the pre-favorite in the race, Jim Peters of Britain, to draw even before asking him in flawless English, "Excuse me, I haven't run the Marathon before but don't you think we ought to go a bit faster?" It was too much for Peters, who dropped out of the race, ostensibly with cramps, not long after Zatopek's query.

It is not surprising that the Helsinki Games were referred to as "the Emil Zatopek Olympiad". Yet his running style was hardly fluid. His gait was uneven and his face often seemed twisted in pain during the course of the race. In the penetrating words of one observer, Zatopek ran "like a man who'd just been stabbed in the heart." It was said that "He does everything wrong except win." In the 1952 Olympics, he was not alone in victory. His wife, Dana, won the women's javelin event, making the Zatopeks the only husband and wife ever to win individual gold medals in a single Games.

UPI/BETTMANN ARCHIVE

Emil Zatopek (left), winner of four distance events, called the Marathon "a very boring race."

The Helsinki Games featured one of the closest races in Olympic history. All of the first four finishers in the 100-meter dash were clocked at 10.4 seconds. The technology was still 12 years away which would time events to the hundreth of a second at the finish line. All that the naked eye saw in Helsinki was four runners breaking the tape at virtually the same moment. After 20 minutes and close examination of the photograph of the finish, the officials declared

America's Lindy Remigino the winner. His right shoulder reached the tape less than one inch before the chest of Jamaica's Herb McKenley. The fourth-place finisher was only a foot behind the winner.

The women's diving competition was not close. Patricia McCormick of the U.S. team won by comfortable margins in both the springboard and platform events. She became the Olympics' first "double-double" winner in diving when, only five months after giving birth to a son, she successfully defended both championships in the 1956 Games. The only other "double-double" diving champion in Olympic history is Greg Louganis, who won from springboard and platform in 1984 and again in 1988. One of Louganis' coaches was none other than Patricia McCormick.

Karoly Takacs of Hungary won the rapid-fire pistol competition in Helsinki. He had won the same event in the 1948 Games. His was a story of triumph over adversity. Takacs in 1938 lost his right (shooting) hand in a military exercise, but this personal disaster did not distract him from taking successful aim on becoming a left-handed Olympic champion.

Nowhere were the triumph and tragedy of the three Olympiads covered in this chapter seen more vividly in combination than in the example of Alfred Schwarzmann of Germany. He was the top gymnast of the 1936 Berlin Games, winning three gold and two bronze medals. His amazing athletic reserves enabled him, 16 years later and at 40 years old, to capture the silver medal in the horizontal bar competition. What he might have achieved in the three Olympiads denied him because of war and Germany's exclusion in 1948 is a haunting question.

The Olympics were visibly slipping on the slopes of ideological rivalry.

At the close of the Helsinki Games, something unprecedented occurred. A nation declared Olympic victory. *Pravda*, the official Soviet newspaper, claimed that Russia had won the Olympics and in doing so had demonstrated the "world superiority" of Soviet athletes. The boast was unseemly and its rationale was strained by any standard. The gold-silver-bronze medals count was 40-19-17 for the United States and 22-30-19 for Russia. The Americans responded with an accounting of their own which argued, also outside the Olympic spirit, that the victory was theirs.

In any event, the Olympics were visibly slipping on the slopes of ideological rivalry. Article 46 of the Olympic Rules ("The Olympic Games are not competitions between nations") was being honored only in the breach. Avery Brundage was swift to issue a warning: "If this becomes a giant contest between two great nations rich in talent and resources, the spirit of the Olympics will be destroyed."

The two super colliders were to be frozen in their contest. The field of competition was to be everywhere. The Cold War would settle in. With it came, in varying degrees, a Big Chill for the Olympic spirit.

Chapter 5

DOWN UNDER TO TOPSY-TURVY, 1956-1984

According to Yogi Berra's Law, "You can observe a lot just by watching." Observation of host cities after mid century tells volumes about the Modern Olympics. The Games for 60 years were held in the cities of Europe and America. The Olympics moved Down Under with the 1956 Melbourne Games. Eight years later, the Summer Games were hosted by Tokyo and in 1968 they were held in Mexico City, the first Olympics in this century in a developing country. Montreal was the host city in 1976. More than half of the Games discussed in this chapter are outside the European or U.S. mold. Old pots were being stirred. The Olympics were part of the broth — and froth.

The chapter might be subtitled in the form of a question: How Did the Modern Olympics Get from Down Under into the Shadows of the Kremlin? The answer: On a serpentine road through political minefields and acts of repression and terrorism, and into a landscape crowded with spectacular athletic achievements. The way from Melbourne to Moscow was a topsy-turvy one.

These were years of contrasts and irony for the Games. The 1964 Olympics, brilliantly organized by the Japanese, were called the Happy Games. The 1980 Moscow Olympics, with almost half of the Olympic community absent through boycott, were known as the Joyless Games. The darkest moment of the period came in Munich, where on September 5, 1972, Palestinian terrorists assaulted Israeli quarters in the Olympic Village, murdered two Israelis and set in motion a chain of events which left 16 people dead. Ironically, the 1972 Games were the most successful ever in terms of athletic performance. Thirty-six world records and 39 Olympic records were set in Munich.

The international reach of television was being felt. There were 100 million television sets in use by 1960 throughout the world, about half of them in the United States. Hundreds of millions of viewers were able to watch segments of the Olympics in Rome and Tokyo by delayed broadcast. After the launch of the first commercial satellite in 1965, live broadcasts were possible from the Mexico City Games, with the added bonus that programs were available in color through ABC-TV, which held the broadcast rights for the 1968 Olympics.

The scale of the Games continued to increase. The Melbourne Olympics in 1956 accommodated over 3300 athletes from 67 countries in programs which included 17 sports and 145 events. The number of Olympians more than doubled by the time of the 1972 Munich Games: 7830 athletes representing 122 countries and participating in 21 sports and 196 events.

Staggering sums of money went into staging the Games. The Germans had spent $30 million to ready Berlin for the 1936 Olympics. They spent almost 70 times that amount for the Munich Games ($2 billion). Japan reputedly spent $3 billion in preparing for the 1964 Olympics. Both nations obviously wished to make economic statements to the postwar world.

The Russians also made a statement. In the seven Summer Games during this period, Russian athletes won 318 gold medals and 797 total Olympic medals. American athletes by comparison won 214 first places and 530 medals overall. However, the United States boycotted the 1980 Olympics in Moscow at the urging, some would say the frenzy, of President Carter.

Still, the athletic message for this period was clear and hardly surprising. Those who are cultivated and supported within a system which uses athletics as *an instrument of national policy* go for the sports yummy with greater intensity and success than those who are not sustained within such a system. Substitute the words "a way to amass wealth" for the italicized phrase in the foregoing sentence and one has a bird's-eye view of professional sports in America. The sports fuel is basically the same for the athlete in both the Russian and American systems. Octane is measured in terms of power, money and recognition. One system, though, is geared for Olympic propulsion and the other for professional performance.

But one can never be smug about computing turns on the Olympic highway. Take the case of Rhodesia, which was excluded from the 1968 Games because of its racial policies. The Rhodesians seemed reform-minded and asked for reinstatement for the 1972 Olympics. The International Olympic Committee in 1971 stated that Rhodesia could participate only if it returned to the conditions which pertained in the 1964 Games; that is, it must compete under the Union Jack as its banner and with "God Save the Queen" as its national anthem. The Rhodesians surprisingly agreed, adding, with African thistles attached, that they would even consent to adopting the Boy Scout emblem in order to participate. Rhodesian athletes, black and white, journeyed to Munich with the blessing of their national Olympic committee. But black African nations, and possibly the Girl Scouts, were not mollified. Rhodesia was excluded anyway in the broad face of threatened boycott by blacks.

What is rich about the indignation against Rhodesia is that 1972 was the same year in which Idi Amin, the rabid-prone dictator of Uganda, forced 50,000 Asians living in Uganda to leave the country, illegally confiscating much of their property in the process. Once the heavyweight boxing champion of Uganda (a title of uncertain tonnage), Amin with brutish fist ordered thousands of the Ugandans who disagreed with him to be killed. Yet no effective opposition to the presence of Uganda surfaced at the Munich Games, a silence all the more interesting given that a Ugandan won the 400-meter hurdles, the first black African ever to win in the hurdles. Indignation can be situational.

Thus did the yellow-brick road run through the Olympics of this period and into the latter decades of a century increasingly fixed on violence and considerations of color. But all was not jaundiced. Transcending the fog of contention and hatred were luminous snapshots of athletes absorbed in personal quests for excellence. For example: four-time Olympic champion Al Oerter defying gravity, age and pain in the arc of his discus toss; Mark Spitz parting the waters in Munich on his way to a single-Games record of seven gold medals; and Nadia Comaneci in 1976 punctuating her movements to perfection above the balance beam. It is they and those like them who give dimension to aspirations

Thus did the yellow-brick road run through the Olympics and into the latter decades of a century increasingly fixed on violence and considerations of color.

and provide direction, even in a topsy-turvy world.

MELBOURNE, 1956: BLOOD IN THE WATER

The idea of Summer Games in December is a foreign one. Unless you are in the southern hemisphere. The Melbourne Games actually were held in the late spring (November 22 - December 8). The atmosphere was troubled.

The British and French had occupied Suez in 1956 after the Israelis attacked Egypt. The Egyptians, along with the Lebanese and Iraqis, withdrew from the Games in protest. Also in 1956, Russia brutally crushed the Hungarian uprising. Holland, Switzerland and Spain withdrew to protest Russia's actions. Avery Brundage, the I.O.C. president, despaired. "In ancient days," he said, "nations stopped wars to compete in the Games. Nowadays we stop the Olympics to continue our wars."

Hard feelings between Russia and Hungary leaked out in Melbourne. The result was blood in the water. The powerful Hungarian water polo team was leading the Russians by the score of 4-0 in the finals when a Hungarian player was cut on the face after a rough exchange. In fairness to the Russians, it must be said that water polo is not canasta. At any rate, the crowd, which included many Hungarian emigres, nearly rioted. The match was ended and Hungary was awarded the gold medal. The Russians at poolside did what had not been done in Budapest. They left.

But other Russian athletes enjoyed enormous success in Melbourne. Vladimir Kuts became only the third person, after Kolehmainen and Zatopek, to win both the 5000 and 10,000-meter races. Kuts also was the first Russian man ever to win an Olympic track-and-field championship. He certainly would not be the last.

Russian supremacy in gymnastics continued. Viktor Chukarin successfully defended his all-around gymnast crown. He and Japan's Sawao Kato (1968 and 1972) are the only men ever to win two gold medals as all-around champion. In the 1952 and 1956 Games, Chukarin won seven gold and three silver medals and one bronze medal.

Australian women made a strong showing in the 1956 Games. Betty Cuthbert won three gold medals in track, and swimmer Dawn Fraser won the first of three successive championships at 100 meters. Fraser is the only Olympic swimmer, woman or man, ever to win the same individual event three times. In the 1960 Olympics in Rome, she carried her mascot, a stuffed koala bear, in the victory ceremonies. Fraser in the 1964 Games bettered her previous winning times and became the first woman to swim 100 meters in less than a minute (59.5 seconds). She is perhaps the greatest Olympian ever produced Down Under. Australia, like Finland and Sweden, has a relatively small population but a robust Olympic tradition.

Because of Australia's strict quarantine laws, somehow a shock to Olympic organizers, equestrian events in the 1956 Games were trotted off in June to Stockholm, which 44 years before had hosted the Olympics.

In Melbourne a Swedish athlete accomplished what was never done before and has never been repeated. Lars Hall won a successive championship in the modern pentathlon. This grueling contest was a favorite of Coubertin and consists of shooting, swimming, fencing, riding and cross-country running. Hall's achievement sets him alongside the canoeist Gert Fredriksson as one of Sweden's best-ever Olympians.

Another Scandinavian set a memorable record in Melbourne. Egil Danielsen set the only track-and-field world record in the 1956 Games with a javelin throw which obliterated the previous best Olympic mark. Danielsen's distance (281 feet, 2 inches) was 39 feet further than any Olympian had ever thrown the javelin. It was the greatest increase over a previous best mark in the history of the modern Games' field events.

Paul Anderson of the U.S. weightlifting team produced no best-ever performance but he got the job done. Anderson, heralded as the Strongest Man in the World, was so intimidating that the Russians did not bother to enter anyone in the super heavyweight division. But Argentina's Humberto Selvetti did enter and he matched the giant from Georgia down to the last grimace. In two lifts, each man put a combined weight of exactly 500 kilograms (1102 pounds) over his head. Neither could do more. It was the only occasion in Olympic weightlifting competition that an exact tie has been recorded. Under the rules of the sport, a tie registers as a win for the *smaller* weightlifter. Tipping the scales at 304 pounds, Anderson was the winner, more svelte than Selvetti by a dozen pounds.

In the medals count by country which is so ardently denounced by Olympic officials, and so closely followed by the entire world, Russia won five more gold medals than the United States (37 to 32) in Melbourne and 24 more medals overall (98 to 74). Russia was the new Olympic juggernaut.

ROME, 1960: THE BAREFOOT PALACE GUARD

The Eternal City had its moments. The 1960 Games began on the 25th day of August, the month named for the Roman emperor Augustus Caesar. Cassius Marcellus Clay was a contestant in the boxing venue. The wrestling venue was in the cavernous Basilica of Maxentius, where in distant prior times Roman grapplers had fought. The Marathon was begun under the majesty of Capitoline Hill, one of the seven hills of ancient Rome and at the mighty heart of the Roman Empire. The race ended, under the light of the moon and torches, near the Arch of Constantine. The winner was one of the emperor's personal guards. The 20th-century Ethiopian emperor, that is.

Abebe Bikila, an Ethiopian soldier, ran barefooted and won by 150 yards over a Moroccan soldier. In a race of perhaps 30,000 strides, the margin of victory was about 80 strides. Bikila won in world-record time: 2 hours, 15 minutes and 16.2 seconds. It was only the third Marathon ever run by Bikila, who insisted that "I could have kept going and gone around the course another time without difficulty. We train in shoes, but it's much more comfortable to run without them."

Bikila, wearing shoes, repeated his victory in the Marathon in the 1964 Games, the only person other than Waldemar Cierpinski of East Germany (1976 and 1980) to win two crowns in this most grueling of Olympic races. Bikila's 1964 Olympic triumph came just five weeks after an operation for appendicitis. He ran again in the 1968 Games but dropped out with an injured leg well before the halfway point. A tragic car accident in 1969 left Bikila unable to walk. He took up paraplegic sports including archery. Dogged by deteriorating health, he died, still young but much diminished, at 41.

Another athlete who excelled in Rome was to die too young. Wilma Rudolph of Tennessee won the 100 and 200-meter dashes and anchored the winning 400-meter relay team for the United States. "Skeeter" to her friends, and "La Gazelle" to the French, she was the 17th of 19 children. Crippled by polio as a child, Rudolph grew up strong of limb to become the first American woman to win three gold medals in Olympic track and field. She died in 1994 before reaching her 55th year.

Rome was afire when Livio Berruti won the 200-meter dash, the first Italian to win an Olympic gold medal in track since 1932. Robert Shavlakadze of the Soviet Union won the high jump and was the first Olympian to clear seven feet (7 feet, 1 inch). A second high-jump milestone was achieved when Romania's Iolanda Balas cleared the bar at six feet, plus one-quarter inch, to win the gold medal for women. She would also take the high-jump crown for women in the 1964 Games. America's Glenn Davis knocked down the 50-second barrier in winning the 400-meter hurdles (49.3 seconds). He had won the event in 1956 as well.

One of the most fiercely contested Olympic decathlons ever staged was won in Rome by Rafer Johnson. He was the silver medalist in 1956. In the Rome Games, he narrowly defeated C.K. Yang of Nationalist China. Both men scored over 8300 points, well above the prior Olympic record. Johnson, like several Olympic standouts before him, later tried his hand at a movie career. He had all the acting ability of a Johnny Weissmuller but not the same luck in swinging successful roles. Johnson was though a formidable decathlete.

Without doubt one of the greatest of modern Olympians was in midpassage of her athletic career in the 1960 Games. Larissa Latynina of Russia was the finest woman gymnast perhaps of all time. She twice won, in 1956 and 1960, the all-around crown for women gymnasts, a feat equaled only by Czechoslovakia's Vera Caslavska in 1964 and 1968. While Caslavska was noted for artistic expression, Latynina was without peer in technical virtuosity. Latynina in Rome won three gold and two silver medals and a bronze medal. She was a gold medalist as well in 1956 and 1964. Her triumphs over the span of three Olympiads were all the more remarkable because she took time out to give birth to two children. During Latynina's reign, she won nine gold medals, more than any other woman in Olympic history, along with five silver and four bronze medals.

MELBOURNE HERALD-SUN

Larissa Latynina of the U.S.S.R. won 18 Olympic medals in her career, more than any other Olympian in history.

Parallel to Latynina's achievement, but on the men's side, was the record of her fellow gymnast and countryman, Boris Shakhlin. From 1956 through 1964, he won a total of 13 medals (7-4-2), the second highest overall number for men in the Modern Olympics. If their first places in the 1956 and 1960 Games were added and represented as the effort of a two-person country team, Latynina and Shakhlin would have placed in the top ten *countries* winning gold medals in each Olympiad! As gymnasts they together won more championships in each of the two Olympics than such countries as Japan, France, Finland or Canada.

Little wonder that the unofficial tally by country in Rome favored Russia over the United States: 43 to 34 in gold medals and 103 to 71 in total Olympic medals. Italy was a distant third in the medals count.

TOKYO, 1964: THE GREATEST UPSET

The Games which began on October 10, 1964, were Japan's first wide opportunity since Pearl Harbor to make a favorable international impression. Olympic officials were also preoccupied with impressions. South Africa was banned from the Games for its racial policies. The Olympic governors who by history had professed to turn a blind eye toward politics hardly blinked in making the decision.

"It will take a miracle for us to be ready in time," said a member of the Olympic organizing committee nine months before the Games were to open. Such fretful expressions have almost become standard among organizers. Sometimes the clock runs out as was the case in Montreal a dozen years later. But Tokyo needed no miracle. Concentrated national purpose and effort sufficed. No detail was overlooked. Avery Brundage was right when he observed that the Japanese "from newsboy to industrial tycoon adopted the Games as his own project and went out of his way to please the visitors." The results have been called the Happy Games.

No one was happier in Tokyo than track team member Billy Mills. The U.S. Marine and part Sioux might easily have been recognized at the Games' start as Dark Horse, if he was recognized at all. The clear favorite in Mills' event, the 10,000-meter race, was the world-record holder, Ron Clarke of Australia. But Mills came out of nowhere at the finish to win by less than a half-second over the silver medalist, a Tunisian. It was probably the biggest upset in the history of the Modern Olympics. Mills' time, an Olympic record at 28 minutes and 24.4 seconds, phenomenally was 50 seconds faster than he had ever before run the race. A numbed Clarke, who placed a close third, was asked if he had underestimated Mills or not worried enough about him. "Worried about him?", Clarke responded. "I never heard of him." Having been introduced, though, it is not likely that Clarke soon forgot Mills. Sudden defeat born by surprise in events of consequence has a way of riveting human memory.

The most courageous moment in the 1964 Games came in the discus event. Al Oerter, the two-time Olympic champion, had fallen and severely injured his ribs. His chest was bound in cumbersome wrapping and he was given a pain-killing injection. To say the least, he was laboring under a disadvantage among world-class competitors. Yet on his next-to-last throw, Oerter uncorked the discus past the 200-feet mark for the first time in the modern Games (200 feet, one and a half inches). "Don't play this up like I'm a hero," he said, "but I really gutted this one out."

UPI/BETTMANN ARCHIVE

Al Oerter is the only modern athlete to win four successive Olympic crowns.

Oerter went on to defend his discus championship again in 1968. No other modern Olympian has ever won four successive gold medals in an individual event. One must go to the sketchy annals of the ancient games to find records comparable to that of the aircraft computer analyst who hurled the disk, as if he had specially designed it, toward the heavens and into history.

Another field-event specialist tried for a fourth successive medal in Tokyo. America's greatest athlete in the shot put, Parry O'Brien, won the event in the 1952 and 1956 Games. He was the silver medalist in Rome. Rising to the occasion in Tokyo, O'Brien made his longest throw ever. But it was not enough. The best that he could manage was fourth place. As Edward Lear, if alive, might have written, champions are beaten down with a cheerful, bumpy sound.

Don Schollander, the best U.S. swimmer prior to Mark Spitz, won four gold medals in the 1964 Games. Like Johnny Weissmuller 44 years before, Schollander won both the 100 and 400-meter races. No other male Olympic swimmer has achieved this double.

Peter Snell of New Zealand also scored a double victory 44 years after it was first achieved in track. Snell, winner at 800 meters four years prior, won both the 800 and 1500-meter races in Tokyo. The two events had last been won by Britain's Albert Hill in 1920. No one since Snell has captured this demanding Olympic double.

The mighty Press sisters on the Soviet team flattened competitors in women's track and field. Tamara Press, winner in the shot put in Rome, won the shot-put and discus events in Tokyo. Her sister, Irina, won the first-ever pentathlon for women with a score never exceeded for the five events. The seven-event heptathlon for women replaced the pentathlon in the 1984 Games. Given the progress of women's sport and its direction, to say nothing of political correctness, the future may well see a full-blown decathlon for women.

The Japanese vaulted over the Russians to gain supremacy in men's gymnastics. Japan won its second successive gold medal in Tokyo in the team combined exercises, a championship which Japan successfully defended five times in all, until 1980 when it did not compete because of the boycott.

The U.S. performance in gymnastics was abysmal in the 1964 Olympics. The highest finish by an American in men's all-around gymnastics was 20th place, while the best that U.S. women could do in their all-around was 34th place.

However, strong U.S. showings in swimming and in men's track and field enabled Americans to claim a slight lead over the Russians at the medals table. The U.S. team held the first-place edge over the Soviets by six gold medals (36 to 30). Americans also led in total medals, 90 to 86.

The lion's share of Olympic medals continued to go to the two contending lions. The lesser cats moved in a different circle. All of which is not to call the Olympics of this period a circus. But neither were they utopia.

> *The lion's share of Olympic medals continued to go to the two contending lions. The lesser cats moved in a different circle.*

Japan earned fourth place in the final standings at Tokyo. A unified German team appeared for the first time in 1964 and took third place. East and West Germany sent separate teams to the Olympics from 1968 through 1988. The two countries reunified in 1990.

MEXICO CITY, 1968: CLENCHED FISTS AND WINGED FEET

The most publicized image of the 1968 Games is that of two American runners giving the Black Power clenched-fist salute from atop a victory stand. The Marquis of Exeter, formerly Lord David Burghley, was not amused: "I will not countenance such action. If anything resembling such a demonstration is repeated, I'll put a halt to all victory ceremonies." No such drastic action was required. The offenders, Tommie Smith and John Carlos, were suspended from the U.S. track-and-field team. They were anything but contrite. They and their idea men, using the term loosely, had no regret about enraging "the elderly millionaires who run the Olympic movement."

Controversy swirled even before the Games began on October 12th. South Africa was banned again from the Olympics even though it agreed to integrate its team. Rhodesia was also banned in a stage setting previously described. Both were denied participation "for real sins it is true," according to one I.O.C. official, "but not without their equivalent elsewhere." The equivalence, actually something more than equivalence, was the Soviet invasion of Czechoslovakia earlier in the year. The large Russian team with its strong column of Olympic hopefuls was not banned.

Ten days before the Games opened, a student protest in Mexico

City drew a crowd of 10,000 people. The Mexican army fired on the students and there ensued a five-hour battle in the tradition befitting a banana republic but not a host city for the Olympic Games. The number of student deaths was put officially at 49. In reality about 260 were killed and 1200 people were injured. The Mexico City Games were then clear to open under the official slogan, *Everything is possible with peace.*

Meeting the Olympic test took on new meaning in the 1968 Games. Tests to confirm the gender of women athletes were conducted for the first time. There were no complaints that these sex tests were in any way underhanded. All athletes were also screened for the first time for use of unauthorized drugs.

Mexico City's 7000-feet elevation helped those athletes accustomed to altitude. The Marathon was won for a third successive time by an Ethiopian, Mamo Wolde. Athletes from mountainous Ethiopia and Kenya won more than half the distance-running events. The thin air also assisted sprinters and field events. Jim Hines of the U.S. team was the first Olympian ever to run the 100-meter dash in less than 10 seconds (9.9 seconds).

Aided by 23% less air density, and with athleticism suggesting a capacity for winged flight, two Olympians recorded spectacular jumps. Viktor Saneev of the Soviet Union launched himself as one of the two greatest jumpers in Modern Olympic history. In the 1968 Games, he was the first athlete to exceed 57 feet in the triple jump (57 feet and three-quarters of an inch). Saneev also was the triple-jump gold medalist in the 1972 and 1976 Olympics. Carl Lewis would later win gold medals in three successive Olympics in the long jump.

But the athlete who most exhibited winged feet in Mexico City was Bob Beamon of the U.S. team. He made what is known simply as The Jump. Beamon smashed the world record in the long jump. The tape measured 29 feet, two and a half inches. Almost two feet further than the old mark. An astounding leap.

The shelf life of Olympic records is not long. Two profoundly important statistics tell all. Olympic records have been broken in about 55% of the finals for track-and-field events in the Games since 1896. The figure is over 70% for swimming! It is unusual for a given record to stand for more than a couple of Olympiads. Jesse Owens' long-jump record in 1936 was an exception. It stood for 24 years until broken by Ralph Boston in the 1960 Games.

Beamon's record is already the longest standing individual mark in the history of the Modern Olympics. Prophecy is treacherous in sports; but The Jump is unlikely to be bettered in the 1996 Olympics, even though Atlanta with its 1000-feet elevation is distinctly higher than most of the cities which have hosted the Summer Games. But elevation is not all-important. The world record for the long jump is held by Mike Powell, who in 1991 surpassed Beamon's mark in non-Olympic competition in Tokyo. Elevation? About 20 feet.

UPI/BETTMANN ARCHIVE

Bob Beamon's long jump in the 1968 Games has proven to be the most durable of Modern Olympic individual records.

The women's 100-meter dash in Mexico City was won by Wyomia Tyus of Griffin, Georgia. Also the winner in 1964, she remains the only woman to defend successfully an Olympic championship in the sprint. On the men's side, Carl Lewis holds this distinction, having won the 100-meter event in the 1984 and 1988 Games.

Japanese men dominated gymnastics in the 1968 Olympics, winning 11 individual medals. On the women's side, the Prague beauty, Vera Caslavska, was in the news. She topped off a stellar career in gymnastics by adding three gold medals to her collection from the 1964 Games. Her 11 Olympic medals (seven gold and four silver) represent the second highest number won by a woman, exceeded only by Latynina. During the Mexico City Games, Caslavska married Josef Odlozil, the Czech silver medalist in 1964 at 1500 meters, in a highly publicized wedding. She then immediately retired from sport.

Gastroenteritis, inflammation of the stomach and intestine, was feared by athletes in Mexico City. It fortunately never materialized as an extensive health threat. Vera Caslavska was also feared by her competitors. Now she was married and out of sport. For the absence of "Montezuma's Revenge" and the reality of Caslavska's Nuptials, many women gymnasts had reason to give thanks.

Americans won 45 gold and 107 total Olympic medals in Mexico City. The corresponding numbers were 29 and 91 for the Soviets. But the view from the top of the hill would be short-lived for the United States.

MUNICH, 1972: THE BEST AND THE WORST OF TIMES

The tale of the Olympic host city of Munich can be summed up in Charles Dickens' familiar opening passage: "It was the best of times, it was the worst of times." The worst came in the last week of the Games when Palestinian terrorists ruthlessly murdered two Israelis in the Olympic Village. The West German police moved decisively but nine Israeli hostages and a policeman were killed, along with five of the eight Arab terrorists. Olympic officials considered suspending the remainder of the Games but decided that international gangsters should not be granted their objective of disruption and intimidation.

Olympic officials considered suspending the remainder of the Games but decided that international gangsters should not be granted their objective of disruption and intimidation.

The Games courageously proceeded, causing the U.S. columnist Red Smith wrong-headedly to complain, "Walled off in their dream world, the aging playground directors who conduct this quadrennial muscle dance ruled that a little blood must not be allowed to interrupt play."

The Olympics which began on August 26th were no mere muscle show. But if the language that columnists themselves popularized were to be used, then it must be recorded that the Russians scored an impressive triple victory. Soviets athletes won Olympic crowns in three categories glibly designated by the media: World's Fastest Human (Valery Borzov, winner at 100 meters), World's Strongest Man (Vassili Alexeev, super heavyweight champion in weightlifting), and World's Best Athlete (Nikolai Avilov, gold medalist in the decathlon).

Borzov won first place in both the 100 and 200-meter sprints. Larry Black, the U.S. runner-up at 200 meters, was not gracious. He volunteered that Borzov owed victory in the 100-meter dash to the fact that a couple of Black's friends had missed the trial heats and therefore were denied what Black described, after a fashion, as certain dominance in the race. What Black did not say was that the U.S. runners missed the trial heats through their own scheduling error. In any event, Borzov's retort ended the street talk. He shrugged and allowed that he "gave about 90 percent of what I had to give."

Running in overdrive in Munich was sufficient for another athlete as well. Lasse Viren won at both 5000 and 10,000 meters without straining himself. But not without falling. The shy village policeman from Finland, the greatest Finnish athlete since Nurmi, fell just before halfway in the 10,000-meter race. Viren got up and finished his run in world-record time. Viren in 1976 successfully defended his championships at 5000 and 10,000 meters, and holds the distinction of being the only runner ever to win both races in successive Olympics.

The 1972 Games saw the end of the longest Olympic domination in an event. For 16 Olympiads, from 1896 through 1968, an American had won the pole vault. Not so in Munich. The event was won by Wolfgang Nordwig of East Germany and he did it with a bang. Nordwig, by the margin of a half inch, was the first athlete in the Olympics to vault over 18 feet.

A more publicized end to an era came with the victory of the Soviets in basketball. The United States had never lost a game in Olympic basketball since the event was introduced in 1936. The Russian win in Munich was among the most controversial in the

Modern Olympics. The U.S. team led 50-49 when the off-court horn sounded the end of the game. The referee, however, ruled that three seconds remained to be played. The clock was restarted and again the horn sounded. Again the referee ruled that, due to alleged confusion, there remained three seconds to be played. The Russians finally succeeded in throwing the ball the length of the court, where a Soviet player astonishingly tipped it into the basket. The victory was given to the U.S.S.R. team by the score of 51 to 50. The Americans were so disgusted that they refused their silver medals.

Mark Spitz in Munich left little to the discretion of the officials. He helped to raise U.S. supremacy in men's swimming, already impressive, to new heights. Spitz won seven gold medals in Munich, a record number in a single Games. He broke or equaled world records 32 times in swimming events throughout his career.

TONY DUFFY/ALLSPORT

Mark Spitz leads modern-day American
Olympians with nine gold medals.

Five of his total of nine gold medals were in relay races, two in the 1968 Games and three in Munich. Nonetheless, his collection of 11 Olympic medals (9-1-1) makes him America's top Olympian in the medals category, with the exception of Ray Ewry whose ten first places, in specialized jumping events (soon discontinued) in the early modern Games, frankly are not comparable, medal for medal, to today's Olympic crowns.

A poster of Spitz in swimming suit and bedecked with seven gold medals was the most popular souvenir of the 1972 Games. Spitz got 15 cents on each poster sale. He was the most celebrated athlete in an Olympics of celebrated athletic achievements.

The sheer scale of Spitz's victories prompted the suggestion by some that swimming events be reduced in the Olympics because of similarities in the events. It is by no means certain, however, that swimming events are disproportionately represented. There presently are 31 racing events in Olympic swimming for men and women, a number roughly comparable, say, to the 28 track events for all Olympians.

Receiving nothing like the adulation given to Spitz in Munich was an athlete who was at least his equal in every respect. Aleksandr Medved of the U.S.S.R. wrestling team won the third of successive gold medals in freestyle wrestling in Munich. In the 1964 Games, Medved defeated Turkey's talented Ahmet Ayuk in the light heavyweight category. Ayuk, from a formidable national wrestling program which has produced dozens of Olympic medalists since 1948, went on in 1968 to win the Olympic crown which Medved previously denied him. Medved moved up to win gold medals as a heavyweight in

NATIONAL WRESTLING HALL OF FAME

One must go back to ancient times to find Olympic wrestlers of the stature of Russia's Aleksandr Medved.

1968 and as a super heavyweight in the 1972 Games. Actually, at just over 220 pounds in Munich, he was the second lightest wrestler in a class of giants. His victims included America's Chris North, a wrestler who outweighed him by almost 200 pounds.

Medved's range and dominance in different categories over the course of three successive Olympics establish him as the greatest heavyweight wrestler of modern times and certainly one of the greatest of all modern Olympians.

The 20-year ritual at the medals table continued when Russia and the United States led all nations in the distribution of Olympic medals. However, for the first time in memory, there was a third and credible contender. East Germany, competing in its first Summer Games, took third place in the unofficial medals count by country. The distribution of total Olympic medals for the now Big Three was 99 for Russia (50-27-22), 94 for the United States (33-31-30), and 66 for East Germany (20-23-23).

The 1972 Games in Munich produced world and Olympic records on a scale not seen before, or since, in the Modern Olympics. Yet the tragic stain left by terrorists on the Olympic fabric would not be easily cleansed.

MONTREAL, 1976: STRIFE AND PIQUE

While the United States was celebrating its bicentennial, its neighbors to the north hosted their first Olympics. The Games which began on July 17th were projected to cost $310 million. Because of labor strife and delays, the final price tag for Canadians was almost five times that amount. Construction on the tower adjoining the Olympic stadium was abandoned until after the Games. Despite attendance of well over three million people, the Montreal Olympics ran a billion-dollar deficit. It was a financial disaster. Few afterward would chance the traditional cheerleader pronouncement that the host city had staged "the best Games ever."

Political headwinds continued to buffet the Games. African nations were up in arms against remote New Zealand. Its illustrious rugby team, ironically called the All Blacks because of their uniform, was touring South Africa which was still an Olympic outcast. Most black African countries objected strenuously and demanded that New Zealand withdraw from the Games. New Zealand's national Olympic committee explained that, while they deplored South Africa's racial policies, the committee had no control over the national rugby team and especially so since rugby was a non-Olympic sport. Black Africans were not satisfied. Twenty-seven African nations boycotted the 1976 Olympics.

The show of pique was not restricted to nations. When two British yachtsmen in the Montreal Games finished 14th among 16 entries in the Tempest class, they made an unambiguous statement of displeasure. They calmly torched their yacht and waded ashore to watch it burn.

After the tragic terrorism in Munich, no effort was spared in Montreal with regard to security. The Games' 24,000 athletes and officials were protected, almost on a one-for-one basis, by 22,000 security people.

But if Olympic participants and attendees were secure, Olympic records were not. The litany of Olympic firsts continued in Montreal. For the first time in the modern Games, a gold medalist had to: throw the hammer over 250 feet (Yuri Syedykh, Russia); throw the javelin with one hand over 300 feet (Miklos Nemeth, Hungary); swim 200 meters in less than two minutes in both the backstroke (John Naber, U.S.) and butterfly (Mike Brunner, U.S.); and swim 400 meters in less than four minutes in the freestyle event (Brian Goodell, U.S.).

When two British yachtsmen in the Montreal Games finished 14th among 16 entries in the Tempest class, they made an unambiguous statement of their displeasure. They calmly torched their yacht and waded ashore to watch it burn.

The most historic first, however, was achieved by a 14-year-old girl from Romania. Nadia Comaneci was the first gymnast in Olympic history to earn a score of 10 across the board in an event. She did it twice for good measure. Comaneci received seven 10's as her scores from seven judges in both the uneven parallel bars and the balance beam. The technical designers of Olympic equipment had not anticipated an athlete of her technical skills. The electronic scoreboard showed nothing higher than 9.95. For Comaneci's performances, it registered only 1.00. The athlete laid words on the heart of the matter in later observing, "it means perfection."

Comaneci won three gold medals and a silver and a bronze medal in the 1976 Games. The Olympic gold medal is not really gold but rather vermeil, that is, gold-plated silver. In a just world, as opposed to one caring too infrequently about perfection, two of Comaneci's first-place medals would have been cast in purest gold.

Other athletes also turned in performances of the first order in Montreal. Japan's greatest Olympian, Sawao Kato, won three gold medals. The diminutive gymnast had won the all-around crown in the 1968 and 1972 Games. In three Olympiads, he garnered 12 medals (8-3-1). Klaus Dibiasi of Italy took the platform diving crown, as he had done in Mexico City and Munich, and thus became the only Olympic diver, man or woman, to defend a championship successfully in three Games. Cuba's Alberto Juantorena achieved in Montreal what no other Modern Olympic runner has been able to accomplish. He won both the 400 and 800-meter track events.

Waldemar Cierpinski of East Germany won the Marathon. He would win the race again in the 1980 Olympics. Cierpinski and Bikila are the only runners to take two gold medals in the Marathon. The East German bettered the winning times of the legendary Ethiopian in each of his victories.

East Germany continued to be the rising star. In fact it was nearing the very top of the Olympic heavens. East Germans won 40 gold and 90 total medals in the Montreal Games, second only to the Russians, with 49 gold and 125 total medals, and ahead of the Americans, who won 34 and 94 medals respectively. East German women won 11 of 13 swimming events.

East Germany used sport as an instrument of national policy. It organized state-sponsored sports schools and training camps in a manner long practiced by the Russians. One East German official in Montreal boasted that their Olympic prowess "proves the success of our socialist system and our training methods." Few knew it at the time but the clock was ticking against this boast.

One Olympian though read its hollowness. John Naber, who spoke with authority having won four gold medals and one silver medal, disagreed: "Gold medals don't mean the White House is better than the Kremlin. It means I swam faster than anyone else, that's all." But state functionaries in the East were not listening. Yet.

Strife and pique were merely in the air in Montreal. They would rain down with such force in 1980 as to threaten to wash away the Modern Olympics.

MOSCOW, 1980: A HOUSE DIVIDED

The Soviet military intervened in Afghanistan in 1979 in much the same way as the United States intervened in southeast Asia 15 years before. President Carter decided to punish the Russians and to make a moral statement by boycotting the 1980 Games in Moscow. The wisdom of Mr. Carter's decision was challenged at the time and continues to raise questions.

Britain did not participate in the 1980 boycott, arguing that, since diplomatic and trade links with Moscow were maintained, an Olympic boycott made no real sense. A Dutch member of the I.O.C. pointed out that "It is unjust to make athletes the conscience of the world." But Carter, unable or unwilling to spear the Soviets otherwise, wanted them on the sports skewer. What followed was an Olympic house divided and the deepest rift yet seen in the modern Games.

Rule 26 of the Olympic Charter states that national Olympic committees "must be autonomous and must resist all pressures of any kind whatsoever, whether of a political, religious or economic nature." Carter was not interested in Rule 26. He had White House aides privately threaten the U.S. Olympic Committee with loss of autonomy. He also threatened legal action, if necessary, to keep U.S. athletes out of the Moscow Games.

President Carter in the end had his way. The United States was joined by West Germany, Japan, China, Canada and others in the biggest boycott in Olympic history. Eighty-one countries sent 6000 athletes to Moscow. Sixty-four nations boycotted the Games which began on July 19th.

Whatever else the effect of the boycott, it did surprisingly little to dampen athletic successes in the Games. The 1980 Olympics produced 47 Olympic and world records, more than any Games before or since, other than those in Munich where a total of 75 records were set.

The Soviets may have spent as much as $10 billion to stage the 1980 Games. It therefore was heavy irony in 1984 when they criticized "commercialization" in the Los Angeles Olympics, the first ever privately financed (at the level of about $500 million). A half million foreign visitors had been expected for the Moscow Games but only about 100,000 showed up. Within the shadow of the Kremlin, though, few cared whether the Olympic ink ran red or black.

The 1980 Olympics are recalled, at least in the United States as the Joyless Games. One reason was the keen disappointment felt by hundreds of American athletes who had spent years in training and preparation. Another reason was the lack of television coverage in Moscow. Americans, who originally expected more than 150 hours of coverage, had to settle for a few minutes each day.

Nevertheless, the sports themselves were filled as always with individual and team superlatives. There were dramatic contests between the world's two best middle-distance runners, Steve Ovett and Sebastian Coe, both of Britain. Befitting an Olympics gone topsy-turvy, Ovett won Coe's best event, the 800-meter race, while Coe won the gold medal at 1500 meters in the race for which Ovett was famous.

Russia's Aleksandr Dityatin became the only man to win an Olympic medal in all eight categories of gymnastics in the same Games. He collected three gold and four silver medals and one of bronze. Perhaps the greatest of Soviet male gymnasts competed in his final Games in 1980. In three Olympiads, beginning in 1972, Nikolai Andrianov won 15 medals (7-5-3), the most awarded to any man in the Modern Olympics.

However, no athlete in Moscow was more talented than Teofilo Stevenson. The Cuban heavyweight boxer won his third successive gold medal in the 1980 Games. In 1972 he gained the Olympic championship in less than six rounds of boxing. Stevenson, over the space of a decade, simply knocked out most of his opponents. He was to boxing what Aleksandr Medved was to wrestling, the greatest Olympic heavyweight of modern times.

There is little doubt that had he chosen to turn professional in 1980, Stevenson would have quickly become a top contender for the world heavyweight title. Many believe that he could have taken the title from Larry Holmes. But idle speculation is easy outside the range of a heavyweight champion's punch.

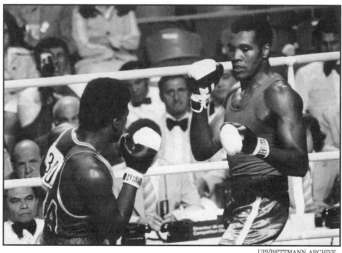

Teofilo Stevenson of Cuba (at right) beat all heavyweight contenders in boxing over the course of three Olympiads.

As for team efforts, the long-time supremacy continued for Soviet women gymnasts in combined exercises. They dominated the event for eight successive Olympiads, from 1952 through 1980, despite breath-taking performances in latter times by Romania's Nadia Comaneci, who won two gold medals in Moscow.

East Germany sent powerhouse teams to the 1980 Olympics, especially in women's swimming and diving in which they won 12 of 15 events. East Germans also prevailed in 11 of 14 rowing categories. Both on and in the water they were indomitable. With a population of only 17 million people, East Germany, for its size, was fielding the most successful individuals and teams in Olympic history. Pretensions of a master race filed away as a shameful memory, the East Germans contented themselves with being masterful Olympians. All at a price of course. Paid not only by the state but also by the athletes themselves in terms of individual liberty.

Pretensions of a master race filed away as a shameful memory, the East Germans contented themselves with being masterful Olympians.

Not surprisingly, half of the Olympic crowns in Moscow went to Russia (80-69-46) and East Germany (47-37-42). Bulgaria placed a distant third (8-16-17). The truth is that, even had the United States competed in Moscow, it probably would have placed only third in the unofficial standings by country.

At the close of the Games in Lenin Stadium, the president of the I.O.C. issued a statement wedged between exasperation and warning. Acknowledging that "sport is intertwined with politics", Lord Michael Killanin cautioned that "sport and the Olympic Games must not be used for political purposes, especially when other political, diplomatic and economic means have not been tried."

Yet who was listening? Apparently not Russia's leaders, already settling into formative thoughts about pay-back time in 1984. This demon would not be stilled, even in the City of the Angels.

Chapter 6

SHOWTIME AND SHOW IT ALL, 1984-1996

The modern Games at times have included events such as mountain climbing, choral singing, dumbbell swinging, still fishing and bowling on the green. More recently the emphasis has been on Showtime. Synchronized swimming was introduced as an Olympic sport in 1984. Its hard-floor equivalent, ballroom dancing, has been tentatively approved as a demonstration sport in the Sydney Games in 2000. The popularity of rehearsed movement and sequins is well established. Next to the Super Bowl, the most watched of all sports programs on American television are the finals of the women's Olympic ice-skating competition.

Television has been the major influence in promoting the Olympics as Showtime. The first TV-coverage rights for the Summer Games were purchased by CBS in 1960 for $394,000. Since then the sale of TV rights for the Games has come to represent one of the chief sources of revenue for Olympic planners. A quantum jump came in 1984 when ABC paid $225 million for coverage of the Los Angeles Games. The TV rights for the Atlanta Games went to NBC for $456 million.

The modern Games at times have included mountain climbing, choral singing, dumbbell swinging, still fishing and bowling on the green. More recently the emphasis has been on Showtime.

NBC in turn will collect vast sums in advertising from Coca-Cola, Kodak, Wheaties and scores of others. Having anted up, though, advertisers do not want viewers channel surfing. The TV eye therefore will focus largely on Olympic events with entertainment appeal. Priority goes also to those venues where Americans

are in the hunt for Olympic medals. Swimming, men's track events, basketball, boxing and tennis will get much more TV coverage than badminton, field hockey, Greco-Roman wrestling, rowing or team handball.

Showtime is the province of professionals and sports personalities. The early Modern Olympics required that all athletes be amateurs in accordance to the Olympic definition. That is, competition was restricted to athletes "to whom participation in sport is nothing more than recreation without material gain direct or indirect". Runners in Nurmi's era were known to bend this rule. Flashy striders in recent times have fractured it beyond recognition.

The arrival and quick successes of the Soviets on the Olympic scene in the 1950s soon made clear that the call for amateurism would be sorely tested. Soviet athletes were state-supported and rewarded lifelong for Olympic triumphs. Olympic gold was assayed in terms of fame but also dachas, income and luxury goods. It takes little genius to forecast what happens when full-time athletes motivated by direct gain compete against part-time athletes motivated by joy of sport.

In 1974, the national Olympic committees were allowed to pay athletes while in full-time training. The athletes receive expenses plus salary equivalents. The contemporary slide toward professionalism was on. In 1981, track and field athletes were allowed to receive money for endorsing products. Other sports followed suit. The I.O.C. in 1983 accepted rule changes by governing member federations that permitted certain professionals to play soccer. It is no coincidence that soccer for many years has been the Olympics' biggest money maker in attendance.

Professionals are now allowed as well in Olympic ice hockey, tennis and basketball. Nothing in the long term appears to insulate other sports, especially team sports, from the tide of professionalism.

Showtime and professionalism reached high tide — ebb tide to some — in the 1992 Games. The U.S. basketball "Dream Team" took the floor. Consisting of 11 multimillionaires and one collegian, the Dream Team was called "the greatest marketing phenomenon since Elvis went on his extended vacation." It was created to make a slam-dunk statement in response to the fact that the American basketball team took only a bronze medal in the 1988 Games. And unlike the disappointment in 1972, there were no alibis in Seoul.

The Russians, indeed the world, needed to be shown how hoops are done. Enter the impenetrable NBA phalanx. The superstars were rich in talent and life styles. Why put up at the Olympic Village when hotel suites in Barcelona were available at $900 per night? The Dreamers played to expectations and demolished opponents by an average of 43 points per game. The crowds loved it. The Dream Team was marketed and bought as fun-loving court magicians rather than NBA bullies. "Magic" Johnson was their leader. They played as Hilton Globe Trotters in a five-ring circus.

> *The Dream Team was marketed and bought as fun-loving court magicians rather than NBA bullies. "Magic" Johnson was their leader. They played as Hilton Globe Trotters in a five-ring circus.*

With the blessings of I.O.C. president Juan Samaranch, the slam-dunk professional has arrived and is heralded on Olympic turf. Got a problem? Wake up and smell the espresso! Right. Or is it?

LOS ANGELES, 1984:
THE OLYMPICS GO TO HOLLYWOOD

The cloud of a major boycott hung over the Los Angeles Olympics even as it had during the prior two Summer Games. The Soviet Union and 13 Eastern bloc nations boycotted the 1984 Olympics, ostensibly to protest "commercialization" and the lack of security for the athletes. The latter reason verged on the absurd. Over 50 independent law-enforcement agencies, including the FBI, maintained security in Los Angeles. The real reason for snubbing the Games was simple revenge for the Carter-led boycott of the Moscow Games.

The Eastern bloc held its own party. Four days after the Olympic flame was extinguished in Los Angeles, the Soviets began the so-called Friendship Games, complete with Olympic-style trappings such as torch procession, award of medals and the playing of national anthems in recognition of victors. The Soviets boasted that the Friendship Games, which were held in six nations, produced athletic records that generally surpassed those in Los Angeles. Anchored by the performances of strong Russian and East German teams, the boast was not an idle one.

President Ronald Reagan opened the Los Angeles Games on July 28th amid swirls of smoke and colors befitting Disneyland choreographers. Hollywood's most recognizable product welcomed the Olympics to the city that had put him on the high track. Reagan was the first U.S. president ever to preside over an Olympic opening ceremony. The vice-president had done the honors 52 years prior in Los Angeles. Vice-presidents extended welcomes also at the openings of two of the three Winter Olympics held in the United States (1960 and 1980). President Theodore Roosevelt's daughter, Alice, managed the reception in the St. Louis Games in 1904.

The 1984 Games were the first in which responsibilities for orchestrating and financing were given not to the host city but to an independent, nonprofit organization. The president of the Los Angeles Olympic Organizing Committee was 46-year-old Peter Ueberroth, a self-made millionaire in the travel industry. He apparently possessed those special twins of genius, knowing when to close the itinerary and when to say no.

The organizing committee's financing came from sale of TV rights, commercial sponsorships and ticket revenues. Ueberroth's masterful plan called for reuse of the 1932 Olympic venues and relied on the superb athletic facilities in southern California. The budget fixed expenditures at about $475 million, more than a 300-fold increase over the $1.5 million tab for the 1932 Games in Los Angeles.

Almost six million people attended the 1984 Games. The revenues from all sources were almost $620 million, which translated to an impressive surplus of nearly $150 million. The surplus was donated to amateur sports, about half going to the U.S. Olympic Committee and its national governing bodies. The 1984 Games were the most successful financially in Olympic history.

The Los Angeles Olympics can be considered a landmark in other respects as well. They saw the first Summer Games participation by Americans subsequent to the 1977 opening of the U.S. Olympic Training Center in Colorado Springs. The center provides state-of-the-art facilities for Olympians readying for competition. Included are a swimming flume that propels water against swimmers (thus providing a type of aquatic weightlifting) and a pressure chamber that simulates high altitudes. But since the elevation of Colorado Springs is 6000 feet, the entire center is indeed geared for high-altitude training.

The 1984 Games saw the high-flying I.O.C. president, Juan Samaranch, for the first time at work with U.S. Olympic planners. Samaranch is something of a stealth-executive. He flies with a virtually invisible trace from camouflaged origins into skies contested by wealthy bidders. He pilots the great circles which are the objects of their interest.

Samaranch is something of a stealth-executive. He flies with a virtually invisible trace from camouflaged origins into skies contested by wealthy bidders. He pilots the great circles which are the objects of their interest.

Samaranch took the controls of the I.O.C. at the close of the Moscow Games. The city was well known to him since he was rewarded after Franco's death by appointment in 1977 as Spain's ambassador to the Soviet Union. Samaranch served well in Franco's pro-fascist Spain in positions from which he oversaw industrial development, financed in large part by fabulous payments from the United States for use of air and naval bases in the country. Samaranch was awarded the Grand Cross of Spain for civil, naval, military, aeronautical and agricultural merit, interests doubtless cultivated, along with accounting, by the former bank president and business director. He is deeply experienced in the ways of sponsors and sponsorship.

In a power play within the I.O.C., Samaranch recently defeated efforts by a majority of members to adhere to age limits concerning his post. Samaranch resorted to late night petitions, changes in balloting procedures, and tactics reminiscent of Catalonian monarchy to continue his rule, if he chooses, into the next century.

The outstanding athlete in Los Angeles was Carl Lewis. At 23 he already was earning a million dollars a year from endorsements made possible under liberalized Olympic rules which, with a straight face, categorized him as an amateur. Lewis lived in a luxurious home in Houston and collected fine china and crystal. He also collected Olympic gold medals. He got four of them in the 1984 Games by repeating Jesse Owens' historic feat at 100 and 200 meters and in the 400-meter relay and the long jump.

Lewis is the greatest Olympian in track since Paavo Nurmi and joins Nurmi and others in the first rank of all-time Olympic greats.

STEVE POWELL/ALLSPORT

Carl Lewis was the first Olympian since Jesse Owens to win four gold medals in track and field in a single Games.

Nurmi and Lewis are similar in several ways. Both excelled in three successive Games. Both won a fistful of Olympic medals. Nurmi collected nine gold and three silver medals while Lewis holds eight gold and one silver. Both courted money. Both shunned the media. They were governed, however, by different Olympic rules. If Lewis is an amateur, then Nurmi was a choir boy.

Lewis, called in Europe the Son of the Wind, expresses a breezy philosophy. "Life is about timing," he says. Carl Lewis should know. He timed his takeoffs perfectly in winning the long jump in 1984 and in the two following Olympiads. He timed his release to perfection in successfully defending the 100-meter championship in the 1988 Games with a world-record sprint of 9.92 seconds. This was the winning time after the first-place finisher, Ben Johnson, failed his drug test.

Another millionaire *amateur* ruled the track with Lewis in Los Angeles. Edwin Moses won the 400-meter hurdles in the 1976 Games. He won the event again in 1984. It was his 105th consecutive victory in the 400-meter hurdles. Moses would have been the obvious favorite in the event in the Moscow Games. The U.S. boycott in 1980 denied him the opportunity to become the only athlete ever to win the same Modern Olympic event in track three times. Four athletes have won an Olympic field event at least three times. Al Oerter won four.

Britain's Daley Thompson won the Olympic decathlon for the second time in Los Angeles. His brashness equaled his athleticism. Before his first championship in Moscow, Thompson

Daley Thompson of Britain won the Olympic decathlon in 1980 and 1984.

announced that "I don't even think about the possibility of not winning — it never occurs to me. I really am that confident." Bravado and a volunteering tongue earned him the title "Muhammad Ali of track". Thompson's confidence in 1980 may have been assisted by the fact that the world-record holder in the decathlon, a West German, did not compete in Moscow because of the boycott.

But Thompson's victory in the 1984 Games proved his mettle. He ran, jumped, hurdled and threw his way to a world record (8798 points) in Los Angeles. His decathlon performance still stands as the Olympic record. Thompson and Bob Mathias are the only athletes ever to win two Olympic decathlons.

In the absence of the perennially powerful Russian team, Romania dominated women's gymnastics. Ecaterina Szabo won four gold medals. Sixteen-year-old Mary Lou Retton of the U.S. team won five Olympic medals in gymnastics, including one gold for the all-around event in which she beat out Szabo by the wispish margin of five one-hundredths of a point.

Even closer were the finals in the women's 100-meter freestyle swimming event. Those finals in fact were the closest in Olympic history, a tie right down to the hundredth of a second. Nancy Hogshead and Carrie Steinseifer, both on the U.S. team, posted identical finishes at 55.92 seconds.

Without the presence of Cuba's tough pugilists, U.S. boxers won 11 Olympic medals in the 12 weight divisions. Americans also enjoyed success in men's gymnastics, wrestling and women's swimming in the absence of Russian and East German favorites. In freestyle wrestling, two brothers from the United States won crowns. Ed Barach won as a light heavyweight and Lou Barach took the heavyweight title.

A few months after arthroscopic surgery on her knee, Joan Benoit of the United States won the first-ever women's Marathon in the Olympics. She finished the race 90 seconds ahead of Norway's Grete Waitz. Benoit's time (2 hours, 24 minutes and 52 seconds) was only a couple of minutes off the pace set by Emil Zatopek in the 1952 Olympic Marathon.

Layered with talent such as that of Michael Jordan and Patrick Ewing, the U.S. basketball team won its ninth championship in ten Olympic outings. The Americans beat Spain, 96-65.

The United States won 174 Olympic medals (83-61-30) in Los Angeles, far more than runners-up West Germany (17-19-23) and

Romania (20-16-17). Wealthy athletes and others in the hunt for endorsements and Showtime exposure led the way in America's dominance in 1984. The year pointed to by title in George Orwell's book was in high summer. Orwell would have recognized the Olympic landscape. His newspeak was afoot for the *amateurs* in the environs of Hollywood.

The year pointed to by title in George Orwell's book was in high summer. Orwell would have recognized the Olympic landscape. His newspeak was afoot for the amateurs in the environs of Hollywood.

SEOUL, 1988:
A SEMBLANCE OF CALM

The 20 years leading up to the 1988 Games were anything but tranquil for the Olympics. All five Summer Games of the period were marred. The 1968 Olympics are remembered for the disruptive acts of Black Power disciples, not to mention the tragic deaths of hundreds of Mexican students gunned down in the streets of Mexico City. Munich conjures up images of the hooded head and bloody hand of terrorism. The Olympics in Montreal, Moscow and Los Angeles were boycotted on a broad scale.

A relative peace returned to the Olympic stage in the 1988 Games, if by this characterization we allow for the presence of 120,000 policemen, the use of metal detectors in Olympic venues and the widespread search of vehicles for explosives. The peace obviously was a fragile one.

North Korea had demanded to cohost the Olympics. North Koreans eventually were offered the opportunity to host five events. They refused and boycotted the Seoul Olympics. The Games proceeded under heavy policing and with U.S. forces in the area on alert in event of disruption, even war, by North Korea. The South Korean government dealt also with serious threats by student extremists. Somehow a peace was maintained. A calmness of sorts was kept in the Land of the Morning Calm. At least there was a semblance of calm.

The U.S. Supreme Court even contributed in a sense to the maintenance of Olympic order. The court ruled, in *San Francisco Arts v. U.S. Olympic Committee*, that the U.S.O.C. has control over all commercial and promotional usage of the word "Olympic" and acted within its authority in stopping homosexuals from staging an athletic event called the Gay Olympics.

South Korea intended to use the Olympics that began on September 17th to show the nation's economic vigor and political maturity. The Seoul Games were to be an affirmative national statement in the same robust vein as intended by the Japanese and Germans in the Olympics of 1964 and 1972. South Korea spent the immense sum of $3.1 billion, over six times the budget for the Los Angeles Games, to insure that its national statement was well articulated and that it was heard. A welcome offspring of the effort was a sharply improved athletic showing by South Korea, which won 12 gold medals in Seoul. That was twice the number won in the 1984 Games.

Two American women track stars captured much attention in Seoul. Florence Griffith Joyner won three gold medals and one silver. Her world-record time at 200 meters (21.34 seconds) was better than the mens' records in 69 countries. Her sister-in-law, Jackie Joyner-Kersee, broke the world record on her way to winning the gold medal in the heptathlon. She accumulated 7291 points in the seven events.

The heptathlon is the women's equivalent to the decathlon. Like the decathlon it is a two-day event. The 100-meter hurdles, high jump, 200-meter race and shot put are featured on the first day, while the second day consists of the long jump, javelin throw and 800-meter race. For the men's decathlon, the 100-meter dash, 400-meter race, long jump, shot put and high jump are contested on the first day, and the second day includes the 100-meter hurdles, discus, pole vault, javelin throw and 1500-meter run. The winners of the heptathlon and decathlon justifiably are often called the world's greatest female and male athletes.

Jackie Joyner-Kersee is perhaps the best woman athlete of all time in track and field. She won the silver medal in the heptathlon in 1984, the year in which it replaced the women's pentathlon. She missed taking the gold medal by just one second in the final event, the 800-meter race. However, she won the heptathlon crown in both the 1988 and 1992 Games to become the first

MIKE POWELL/ALLSPORT

Jackie Joyner-Kersee virtually has owned the seven-event Olympic heptathlon since it replaced the women's pentathlon in 1984.

Olympian of either sex to win multi-event medals in three Olympics. She also broke the Olympic record in winning the women's long jump in 1988.

As an 18-year-old in the 1980 Olympic trials, Joyner-Kersee failed to make the U.S. team in the long jump. "I went home crying," she says. Most of the weeping afterward, though, would be that of her disappointed opponents. She was coached in the 1988 Games by her husband, Bob Kersee.

The most notorious incident of the 1988 Games was in the 100-meter dash. Ben Johnson of Canada ran the event in the incredible time of 9.79 seconds, beating his own world record. But he failed the post-race drug test. Traces of banned anabolic steroid, a muscle-building drug, were found in Johnson. Therefore, the gold medal went to runner-up Carl Lewis, whose time also broke the world record. Ten athletes tested positive for drugs during the Games, including three gold medalists.

The boxing venue was the site of another controversy. The American light middleweight, Roy Jones, beat Korea's Park Si-hun by a comfortable margin, at least to the visible eye. Going into the third and final round, Korean television announced that Park would need a knockout to win. He did not get it or anything close to it. But he did get the decision. In a confounding move by the mysterious East, Park was declared the winner by a 3-2 margin. There is subjectivity and there is error. The decision was the latter by near-universal agreement.

The most dramatic moment of the Seoul Games came in the water. More accurately, in the air above the water. The drama was provided by Greg Louganis, the greatest Olympic diver in history. Of Samoan and northern European ancestry, Louganis was

Greg Louganis punctuated the water and the air above it with clearest art.

adopted at an early age. He took up gymnastics to combat asthma and then progressed to diving. He was the silver medalist in platform diving in Montreal. The winner of almost every major diving championship in the 1980s, Louganis would have been the clear favorite in the Moscow Games. He took the Olympic diving "double" in the 1984 Games as winner of both the springboard and platform events.

Tense drama in the 1988 Games unfolded with Louganis' final platform dive. He trailed a brilliant 14-year-old challenger from China and needed a near-perfect score to keep his title. Louganis nailed it to retain the platform championship by the micro-spray margin of 1.14 points. He again won the Olympic diving "double", joining Patricia McCormick (1952 and 1956) in an elite, two-person category.

Louganis in 1995 announced that he has AIDS (acquired immune deficiency syndrome). He was known by a few to be HIV positive prior to the 1988 Games, which caused something of a delayed furor because Louganis hit his head on the springboard during the competition in Seoul. The scalp wound required four stitches.

There was a well-publicized instance of blood in the water during the water polo finals of the 1952 Olympics. But Louganis' experience exposes a new dilemma. His case and that of "Magic" Johnson, a 1992 Olympian who declared himself to be HIV positive well prior to the Games, pose unsettling questions. Where do the rights of the HIV-carrier to pursue a *normal* life lead, especially where do they lead in sport? If Olympians can be tested for drugs for the sake of sport, should they be tested for HIV for the sake of fellow competitors and the officials? The I.O.C. is likely to duck the issue for as long as possible. It is doubtful, however, that a duck and don't tell policy will be acceptable for the long term.

> *If Olympians can be tested for drugs for the sake of sport, should they be tested for HIV for the sake of fellow competitors and the officials?*

Two giants of Olympic swimming scored memorable triumphs in Seoul. The first, almost literally a giant at 6' 8", was America's Matt Biondi, whose Olympic medal tally for an American is exceeded only by that of Mark Spitz. In the three Olympiads from 1984 through 1992, Biondi won 11 medals (8-2-1). He won five gold medals in Seoul, including individual crowns in the 50 and 100-meter freestyle races. He broke the world record in the former and the Olympic record in the latter.

Kristin Otto of East Germany won six gold medals in swimming in the 1988 Olympics, the most ever by a woman in a single Summer Games. Otto's remarkable achievement included four individual championships, the 50 and 100-meter freestyle and 100-meter victories in the backstroke and butterfly events. Kristin Otto and Dawn Fraser perhaps have the strongest claims to the title of best-ever woman Olympic swimmer. At least at this writing. What the cynic said of promises applies as well to Olympic records and claims for best-ever Olympian. They are like pie crusts, meant to be broken.

Tennis, dormant as an Olympic sport since 1924, made its return in Seoul. The men's championship was won by Miloslav Mecir of Czechoslovakia. Called by some the Big Cat for his fluid movement, he was unknown to most of the public. Mecir for a brief season was especially hard on young Swedes. The women's gold medal in 1988 went to Steffi Graf of West Germany, who was known to all as the world's premier professional in the women's ranks.

David Robinson could not save the American basketball team from defeat. They finished third, the worst showing since the game became an Olympic sport in 1936. The Soviets beat Yugoslavia in the finals.

Neither could deep talent and a flashy style save the Brazilian soccer team, which finished second to the Soviets in the Seoul Olympics. This was a continuation of bad luck for South America, which produces renowned World Cup winners yet has not enjoyed victory in the Olympics for almost 70 years. The Olympic Games and the World Cup competition are by far the two titans of international sports events. The first World Cup championship was played in 1930 in Uruguay, home to the then-reigning Olympic champions and the only country outside Europe to win the Olympics (1924 and 1928). The Olympic drought for South American soccer could be broken in Atlanta.

Soviet women in 1988 returned to their supremacy over team combined exercises in gymnastics, a dominance which has no equal in the history of the Modern Olympics during the last half century. Russia won the event again in 1992. Only in 1984, when the Soviets boycotted the Games, has another team (Romania) managed to win the women's team combined exercises. Russian women otherwise have ruled the competition since 1952, the first Modern Olympics in which the Soviets competed.

Soviet athletes in Seoul returned to their accustomed place on the Olympic victory stands. The Soviet Union won 132 medals (55-31-46). East Germany was second (37-35-30) and the United States followed closely (36-31-27). But the 1988 Games would be the last for both Russians and East Germans under their traditional banners. Even as events were at work to stitch together again the Olympic fabric, events of a different stripe were in movement which would rip the Eastern bloc asunder.

BARCELONA, 1992: SPECTACULAR GREETINGS AND LAST HURRAHS

Berlin was chosen in 1931 over Barcelona to host the 1936 Olympics. The Germans got the Olympic Games; the Spanish got Guernica. Fifty-five years after the ruthless destruction of Guernica by German air forces in Spain's civil war, the Olympics came to northern Spain and its chief city, Barcelona. The opening ceremonies of the Barcelona Games on July 25, 1992, included a spectacular finale. A disabled Spanish archer shot a flaming arrow from the darkened floor of the Olympic stadium. The arrow arced more than 200 feet into a wall of gas to ignite the Olympic torch in a cauldron on the stadium rim. A parade of Olympic spectaculars was underway, accompanied by a few last hurrahs.

The 1992 Games were the most extensive in Modern Olympic history:

Summer Games	Nations	Athletes	Sports
1992	**172**	**10,563**	**25**
1988	160	9,421	23
1984	140	7,078	21
1952	**69**	**4,925**	**17**

The figues for 1992 represent profound increases over those 40 years prior in Helsinki: two-and-a-half times the countries participating, over twice the number of athletes, and half again the number of Olympic sports.

The performance of the Unified Team in Barcelona was both trumpet call and swan song. The Soviet Union had disintegrated and with it the national team. In its place at the 1992 Olympics appeared the Unified Team, a patchwork of 12 former Soviet republics such as Belarus, Russia and Ukraine. The Unified Team led all others by winning 112

The performance of the Unified Team in Barcelona was both trumpet call and swan song.

Olympic medals in Barcelona. However, the Soviets' mastery of the Modern Olympics for much of a 40-year period was ending.

By 1993 each of the 12 former Soviet republics had formed its own national Olympic committee.

The end came more abruptly for the East German Olympic machine. With reunification in 1990, a single national German team traveled to Barcelona. It took third place in the medals count. But its Olympic mark of 82 medals was still 20 fewer than East Germany alone won in Seoul. East Germany has sounded its last hurrah, but for a unified Germany there is much in the Olympic future about which to cheer.

The most cheered athletes in Barcelona were members of the U.S. basketball team, the so-called Dream Team. Opposing teams looked at contests with the Americans as mere photo opportunities, victory against the NBA's elite being out of the question. The Dreamers gave Croatia nightmares in the championship, 117 to 85. The U.S. team members accepted their medals wearing Reebok tracksuits; but Michael Jordan, Charles Barkley and Magic Johnson, all under contract with Nike, draped American flags over their shoulders to hide the Reebok logo. A show of corporate patriotism.

The Dreamers' coach, Chuck Daley, described his affiliation as like "traveling with 12 rock stars". Cuba's basketball coach too likened them to a star, the sun. After seeing his team blown out by 79 points, he mused: "We have a saying in Cuba. One finger cannot cover the sun."

Cuba was more successful in boxing and baseball. The latter was played for the first time as an official Olympic sport. Cubans won seven gold medals in the 12 divisions of boxing. The Cuban baseball team leveled all opposition, beating the United States 6-1 in the semifinals and Taiwan 11-1 in the finals. Because of boycotts, the Barcelona Olympics were the first for Cuba since 1980. Also returning to the fold in Barcelona was South Africa, after an absence of 32 years.

The most spectacular individual achievement of the Games was that of the Unified Team's Vitaly Scherbo in gymnastics. He led all Olympic competitors by far in winning six gold medals, including five individual medals. Among these was the all-around crown. Scherbo with reason was called a "one man gold rush".

Scherbo was asked whether in the future he would compete for Belarus or perhaps another country. He pulled no punches in responding, "wherever I can make the most money". A writer for the U.S. Olympic Committee accepted the remark without discomfort, referring to it merely as "accurately reflecting the modern-day reality of sport and the Olympic Games."

Pretensions were also absent in the views expressed by 19-year-old Yevgeny Sadovyi of the Unified Team, the only triple gold medal winner in swimming in Barcelona. "Before," he said, "we had to win for the government, for politics. The freedom we now have can lead us to making very good money for ourselves." He assured that "All athletes respond to this motivation." He may be right.

ALLSPORT

Vitaly Scherbo of Belarus is the only Olympian ever to win six gold medals in gymnastics in a single Games.

It is not surprising to hear the above views. Athletes of the former Soviet Union live in a wrecked economy. Olympians on the Unified Team were paid $3000 for each gold medal, a huge amount in the desperate markets of the republics. It is understandable that Scherbo and others seek to protect, even enrich, themselves financially.

But one person's hedge is another's greed. The expressions of what some might call greed by Scherbo and Sadovyi go unchallenged in Olympic quarters. They are accepted apparently with wink and smile. The Olympics are dropping all pretenses. There now is open acceptance of professionals for hire, a transformation which took centuries for the Greeks. An emblem of modern times and swift change.

There is nothing in this movement which is inconsistent with the overall approach of the present Olympic leadership. There is little that is not subject to sale or licensing. When the trough is gilded at the top, the urge to wade in with all four feet finds its way to the playing field.

Yet moral indignation has its limits. The Dream Team was not forced on anyone. It is worth remembering that the gimmick, or stroke of genius, was probably the most spectacular feature of a highly successful Olympics. There seems to be no ground swell in favor of reforming the Olympic Movement. The Circus Maximus was built without protest.

The economic incentive appears to have worked with Spain's Olympians. The host country in the Olympics usually improves its past performances. The improvement for Spain in 1992 was remarkable. The Spanish won a single gold medal in Seoul. In all Summer Games prior to 1992, Spain's athletes won only four Olympic crowns. Spaniards won 13 gold medals in Barcelona. Many winners doubtless were motivated by the offer of a Spanish bank to pay a million dollars to every Spanish gold medalist. The stipend begins at age 50 for the athlete and is to be paid in monthly installments.

Not without reason has Barcelona for centuries been famous as a trading center in the Mediterranean.

Money, however, did not always deliver the goods in 1992. Consider Nike's Dave-and-Dan fiasco. Nike spent $25 million to advertise the Olympic decathlon as a foregone conclusion, a two-man contest between Americans Dave Johnson and Dan O'Brien. Both handsomely outfitted (and paid) by Nike. But Nike forgot to tell the officials conducting the U.S. trials for the Olympics. O'Brien did not even make the team. Johnson, suffering a foot stress fracture, limped only to a bronze medal in the decathlon in Barcelona. Robert Zmelik of Czechoslovakia was unannointed by Nike but he accepted the gold medal anyway.

Dave Johnson's route to Barcelona was instructive. He attended Azusa Pacific, a small Christian college in California. To assist his Olympic preparations, the U.S.O.C. got him a job, ironically with Budweiser. Johnson explained his dilemma and decision to take the job: "That was tough because of my faith. But we came to the conclusion that it was a need being met." It is no commentary against Johnson personally to observe that the Olympics and times in general are much changed since Eric Liddell for religious reasons refused to race on a Sunday in the 1924 Games.

Five athletes, three of them Americans, tested positive for drugs in Barcelona. Ten athletes failed drug tests in Seoul. But Olympic officials could hardly be smug about progress. The U.S.O.C. thought it necessary to issue a poster warning that "Olympic Glory Is For Athletes Not Addicts". All three Olympic medalists in the shot put in Barcelona had served suspensions for previous use of drugs which enhanced performance.

Nowhere has drug testing in the Olympics been felt more keenly than in the weightlifting venue. There were many world and Olympic records broken in weightlifting in Seoul. The Barcelona Games saw no world records and only two Olympic records. Stricter drug testing was having the desired effect. Athletes were depending on adrenaline not steroids.

One world record was produced in individual events in track and field in the 1992 Games. Kevin Young broke the world record in the 400-meter hurdles with a time of 46.78 seconds. Carl Lewis won the long jump in an upset victory over the world-record holder, Mike Powell. Only Carl Lewis and Jackie Joyner-Kersee at Barcelona successfully defended championships won in individual track-and-field events in the 1988 Olympics.

The biggest upset of the 1992 Games was in the pole vault. The Games' overwhelming favorite was the 1988 gold medalist. But Sergei Bubka of the Ukraine failed to clear any height at all in Barcelona. It was as if Tarzan had forgotten how to swim. The pole vault was won by a fellow Unified Team member, Maksim Tarasov, who cleared the bar at 19 feet and one-quarter inch.

Both Bubka and American decathlete Dan O'Brien partially redeemed themselves in sport later in the summer of 1992. Possibly driven by their earlier failures, both athletes set new world records. Bubka cleared 20 feet, one and a half inch. That brought his career total for world records in the pole vault to an unprecedented 32. O'Brien defeated Olympic champion Zmelik in decathlon competition in Talance, France. O'Brien's world-mark performance was for a total of 8891 points. The Nike wars behind him, O'Brien wore a Reebok shirt in the competition.

The top three teams by medals count in the 1992 Summer Games were:

	Gold	Silver	Bronze	Total Medals
Unified Team	45	38	29	112
United States	37	34	37	108
Germany	33	21	28	82

What the above table does not show is that the Unified Team's results dissolve for future purposes. If the performances of the 12 republics are considered individually, the most successful was Russia with 16 gold medals. That was the same number won by China. Neither does the table show that China's total medals count in Barcelona was 54, almost double its number of Olympic medals in Seoul.

Prior to the show-biz closing ceremony in Barcelona, organizers announced that the Games would make a profit of about $5 million. Olympics run so often in red ink that any indication of profit will not readily be challenged. The announced profit is less than one percent of what the Barcelona Games were reputed to attract in corporate sponsorships alone, about $700 million according to one source. By announcement, the organizers were very close to the margin but narrowly on the correct side of it.

A record number of 64 nations won Olympic medals in Barcelona, 12 more than in Seoul. Future Olympics will see a powerful U.S. team intact, a German team well capable of first-place standing, and increasingly strong challenges from China, South Korea and perhaps Japan.

It telling about our expectations that controversy of sorts was stirred when *only* one individual world record was broken in Barcelona for track and field. Extraordinary performances have become ordinary Olympic fare. Our expectations of the Olympic smorgasbord have become bloated. Not every offering can be, nor should it be, the richest ambrosial dessert. Sometimes the robust if plain chocolate or vanilla must suffice. One can survive on such choices.

The Olympic pie of the future will be divided into more pieces. The good news is that it will be a bigger pie.

Chapter 7

ATLANTA AND THE CENTENNIAL GAMES

There are two things that must be understood at the outset about the 1996 Summer Games in Atlanta. They are largely the product of the vision and drive of one man. Next, Atlanta got the Games the old-fashioned way. It earned them. There is much though that needs to be added.

William Porter Payne, a man of inordinate grin and energy, is chiefly responsible for bringing the Olympics to Atlanta. He assembled the players who knew how to pitch to those unaware that Peachtree is a street. Payne is "Billy" to his friends, among whom he would urge the inclusion of the media and a couple of million other people in Atlanta. He projects a sunny presence, the type well pressed in Downtown gatherings of Rotary and Kiwanis. One suspects too a wide vein of craftiness, the kind that works in a favorite refrain twice during a newspaper interview. For example, "spirit is where the strength of Atlanta lies."

Billy Payne's vision has done as much to alter the way Atlanta sees itself as any since that of "Uncle Billy" Sherman 130 years prior. The full nature of the glow and its longevity are yet to be determined.

Billy Payne's vision has done as much to alter the way Atlanta sees itself as any since that of "Uncle Billy" Sherman 130 years prior. The full nature of the glow and its longevity are yet to be determined.

Atlanta earned its place as host city. A good work ethic, of course, does not preclude a capacity for study and strategy, even connivance or intrigue. It would be difficult to convince the city of Athens that there was no intrigue in Atlanta's selection as host for the Centennial Games.

Many indicators pointed to Athens as the likely site to celebrate a full century of the modern Games. Athens was host to the first Modern Olympics. Greece is the mother of the Olympics. Athens seemed the logical choice for the 100th anniversary of Coubertin's dream come true. But the only Athens in the 1996 Olympic picture is Athens, Georgia. It will host the Games' rhythmic gymnastics, volleyball and the soccer finals.

Atlanta had its own approach from the start. "Atlanta never wanted to be the favorite," recalls one planner. Organizers instead worked to cultivate friendships among the I.O.C. members who would make the decision. The city would bide its time. And point to the "social and economic ills that ... had ruined the splendor of Athens."

In best Southern tradition, Atlanta eventually managed to host 68 of the I.O.C.'s 88 voting members. The mayor of Atlanta, Andrew Young, was named as chairman of the city's Olympic organizing committee. The quick hands of former football player Billy Payne were everywhere in the background. The game plan assumed that there were many I.O.C. voting members in what is called the Developing World who would prove initially sympathetic to any reasonable proposal from Young. The idea of Atlanta as host to the 1996 Olympics might have been improbable to some but it was hardly unreasonable.

Young as mayor had expressed an occasional antipathy for what he termed "smart-ass white boys", but these outbursts from an often affable politician did little to damage his credentials among I.O.C. members within target.

Young and Atlanta's new mayor Maynard Jackson were among a delegation of 300 Georgians who traveled to Tokyo in 1990 for the I.O.C.'s General Session and the vote on the 1996 host city. Coca-Cola executives were also in the delegation. The company, headquartered in Atlanta, was in a sensitive position. With worldwide resources and clientele, Coca-Cola did not want to be accused of undue partiality.

THE COKE CONNECTION

Billy Payne from the beginning understood the importance in

Atlanta of Coke's seal of approval. He recalls, "I figured most good things that get done in this community have very much a history of being supported by the Coca-Cola Company." But nothing too overt was possible. The giant company consistently has articulated its role as "statesmanlike". Yet Coca-Cola Plaza is in Atlanta as opposed to Australia. Something might be done for Payne and his Atlanta bid. The Atlanta plan got a crucial boost in 1988 with a cash infusion made possible by the right words from Coke's top executive, Robert Goizueta.

Payne went to Coca-Cola Enterprises, the Atlanta-based bottler, for ongoing support. He got a $250,000 contribution. Coca-Cola bottlers in the other cities seeking the Olympic nod, Athens, Toronto and Melbourne, provided smaller contributions to their hometown bids.

The Georgia delegation in Tokyo expected a deadlock in the early rounds of I.O.C. voting. They were not disappointed. Atlanta was selected by a vote of 51 to 35 over Athens on the fifth I.O.C. ballot. What followed, on Coca-Cola's part, was more suggestive of a victory party than "statesmanlike" posture. The scene was well summarized by an Atlanta journalist:

> Coca-Cola's carefully cultivated image of impartiality crumbled when, moments after Atlanta was awarded the Games in Tokyo, Gary Hite, the company's worldwide sports chief, enthusiastically took to the stage passing out Cokes to the stunned victors. His staff raced around passing out Atlanta Olympic pins adorned with a Coke logo.

> They stopped in their tracks when they saw the stunned expressions of the Greeks, who immediately charged that Coca-Cola had stolen the Games from Athens, which they considered the rightful home of the Centennial Games.

The 1996 Summer Olympics could be called the Coke Games. The company is spending a vault of money, about $200 million, on Olympic sponsorship, advertising, promotion and hospitality. Coke's visibility during the Games will be unmatched by any other company, though that visibility will not be as towering as at first planned.

The Atlanta Olympic committee proposed nine-story high "megasigns" for Coke and sponsors equally liquid to use in advertising during the Games. Although the plan drew fire from environmentalists and advertisers without megasigns, it was rubber-stamped by the Atlanta city council. A federal judge, however, struck down the city ordinance for singling out "particular forms of expression for special treatment." Special treatment, of course, is what premier Olympic sponsors like Coca-Cola are paying for and is precisely what they expect.

The tip of a dangerous iceberg is incidentally revealed here. If authors of books can be held up and required by federal law to pay the U.S. Olympic Committee for the privilege of merely writing about the Olympics, and this is the case as mandated *by law*, why should not Olympic committees become bold in attempts to skew other laws to advantage themselves and favored clients? Is this the bottom line with the Olympics? If so, is it not a movement gone amuck?

These are cold and hostile waters. They will not be tamed in this space. It might be argued, though, that Olympic committees make it their business to do exactly what the federal judge in Atlanta said they may not do. They systematically require, under law, that anything dealing with the Olympics be singled out as "particular forms of expression for special treatment." We supposedly live in the world's most free society but the word "Olympics" cannot even be printed in a book, the subject may not be written about, without permission and payment. Fortunately, the word *amuck* has not yet been licensed.

> *We supposedly live in the world's most free society but the word "Olympics" cannot even be printed in a book, the subject may not be written about, without permission and payment. Fortunately, the word amuck has not yet been licensed.*

It is questionable whether the U.S.O.C.'s policy on licensing books could withstand a stiff challenge on the grounds of free speech.

But back to refreshments. Coca-Cola's Olympic plans include the construction of a $20 million entertainment complex in downtown Atlanta. The games park is intended "to bring the Olympics to the people whether or not they have a ticket to go to an event." This may be taken to mean that

Coke is building the complex in large part for the youth of urban Atlanta.

Coke's Olympic City will treat 9000 visitors at a time to "virtual"-type games. The menu will allow such experiences as simulated basketball play against a "virtual" Dream Team. There will be a simulated velodrome to test cycling skills. Also on the broad menu is a "You Be the Judge" interactive theather in which game players view actual Olympic footage, grade performances and compare scores with those of the real judges.

Ray Bradberry's book *Fahrenheit 451* as science fiction forecasted a type of "virtual" participation. Coke's modern Olympic City, though, will be *cooler* in several respects. Two immense air-conditioned tents will house thrill seekers. The games complex will cover two large city blocks immediately north of the planned Centennial Olympic Park.

The Centennial Olympic Park is not a Coke project but is the subject of considerable hype. Heralded by Atlanta organizers as

Atlanta prepares for the 1996 Games.
Coca-Cola headquarters is the large building at the upper right.

the rival of London's Hyde Park (615 acres) and New York's Central Park (840 acres), the 21-acre Atlanta space is planned as the chief gathering place for crowds during the Games.

There is speculation that Coca-Cola will give its Olympic City property to Atlanta after the Games. This would be consistent with the company's proud record of civic responsibility to the city.

There is little speculation, however, about Coca-Cola's financial position in the Olympics, present or future. As an I.O.C. vice-president expressed, "No matter where the Games are, Coca-Cola will be there."

The Coke connection has a Spanish axis for Olympic purposes. The Games' line between Spain's Juan Antonio Samaranch and Coke's top executive, the Cuban-born Robert Goizueta, should not be underestimated. Both are shrewd in business and diplomacy. Both believe that success can depend on secret formulas. Both know what will go down.

THE BIGGEST THING EVER IN CONYERS

The Atlanta Olympics will fuel Georgia's economy with over $5 billion according to a 1992 study by the University of Georgia. Everyone wants part of the action. Many of them are getting it. In Coweta County, 45 minutes south of Atlanta, businessmen are compiling foreign-language brochures. Bubba is going bilingual.

Bubba is going bilingual.

The Olympics are described as the biggest thing that will ever happen in Conyers, a town 30 miles southeast of Atlanta. Conyers is hosting the equestrian and modern pentathlon events. It is also to be the site of a new Olympic event, mountain biking. The sport has nothing to do with mountains (Conyers is on the Piedmont Plateau). Instead, the cycling is done over rough terrain, a type of obstacle-course race.

The Atlanta Olympic committee is spending $20 million to build venues in Conyers. The town itself is spending almost $70 million for development, including roads and a 100-room hotel. Great expectations attend great events. As a Georgia county commission official sees it, "There is some long-term potential that someone may, for example, come to Conyers, have a good experience at McDonald's and ultimately come back and put an investment there."

Expectations are on the rise as well in Atlanta. Take for instance urine samples. Atlanta University's Morehouse School of Medicine is to receive $1.5 million to analyze 5000 urine samples from athletes during the Games. All medalists and other athletes chosen at random are to be tested for banned drugs. The "research program" by Morehouse will be conducted in cooperation with a commercial laboratory, SmithKline, which will do virtually all of the actual testing. The medical school is to get $300 for study of each urine sample. The expression gold flow may take on new meaning. The school is headed by Louis Sullivan, the former Secretary of Health and Human Services.

Much of Olympic construction in Atlanta is being allotted on an affirmative-action basis. For example, 37% of the work on the Olympic stadium must be done by businesses owned by minorities or women.

Expectations can be subjective and do not always carry a dollar sign. Responding to a question about what legacy he hoped to be left by the Games, then-mayor Maynard Jackson in 1993 probably answered for many of Atlanta's blacks: "I think without question that the memory of Dr. Martin Luther King Jr. is marching alongside the dreams for these Olympic Games." There doubtless also are others in Atlanta, of all colors, who hope, in good faith equal to that of Mr. Jackson, that the city's Olympic reception is not too Afro-centric.

WHAT THE NUMBERS SAY

The Atlanta Games are announced to be on track and within budget. Price Waterhouse accountants state that they find no reason to doubt that the Atlanta Olympic committee will not make its $1.58 billion revenue forecast. Beware the double negative. Not to doubt an absence of failure is not quite the same as saying forthrightly that success is expected. But such is the trade language of accountants, nurtured within the shadow of lawyers and adaptive to the spinning of chameleonic phrases.

The Atlanta Olympic committee may be on target. However, even if it is as yet wide of the mark, one hardly expects a public wringing of hands. Nor, in today's world, candor. There are though a few bothersome signs.

The committee did not issue its first-quarter financial report in early 1995. It also announced that the year's second quarter would not be publicly reported but that a report would come in the fall. The finance chairman's explanation was not the language of clarification: "We just felt that to go through that exercise now was really meaningless."

Figures in early 1995 showed that the committee had raised about $840 million with $740 million remaining to be raised. That meant that about 53% of revenues were committed or in hand. By the spring of 1995, the committee said that revenues had increased to 72% of the $1.58 billion needed. A gap of $438 million reportedly remained.

Calculations are tricky without actual financial reports but logic points to possible problems. The committee is said to be looking for $438 million, the largest part of which is an anticipated $260 million in ticket sales. Even if there is perfect success in this major category of ticket sales, and even if the committee is successful as well in raising half the amount in ancillary categories as raised in the major one, the total comes only to $390 million. That is $48 million short of the amount needed to close the reported gap.

But there are reasons, aside from Murphy's Law (if anything can go wrong it *will*), to doubt that Olympic organizers are to experience near-perfect success. The Olympic committee sold U.S. television rights to the Games for $170 million less than was at first projected. Corporate sponsorship sales are described as "brisk"; however, it appears that the 1996 sales target of $370 million will be far less than the amount reputedly raised in corporate sponsorships by Samaranch (as much as $700 million) for the Barcelona Games.

The sale of Centennial Olympic Park commemorative bricks, although a relatively small source of revenue at $20 million, is going over with a thud. How representative is the brick program? Will the Olympic coin program, which once was looked to for as much as $100 million in revenues, follow a similar trajectory?

Perhaps the area of greatest concern is the ticket sale program. The anticipated sale of 6.8 million tickets seems highly optimistic. Neither the Los Angeles Games nor those in Barcelona, both remarkably successful Olympics, approached this level of ticket sales. Some four million Atlanta Games tickets are said to be already set aside for national Olympic committees, sponsors and hotels. The Olympic committee in late 1994 projected ticket sales at $226 million. Now it says it will raise (or needs to raise) $260 million in ticket sales.

Even using Olympic planners' own figures for projected attendance raises serious questions. For example, planners anticipate Olympic attendance at 59,000 on Day 1, going to 325,000 by Day 7, and peaking at 600,000 on Day 11. Following what seems a rational scenario with these numbers, one gets something like the below schedule.

	Day of Games	Estimated Paid Attendance
Friday, July 19	1	**60,000**
	2	200,000
	3	225,000
	4	250,000
	5	275,000
	6	300,000
Thursday, July 25	7	**325,000**
	8	400,000
	9	500,000
	10	550,000
Monday, July 29	11	**600,000**
	12	500,000
	13	400,000
	14	300,000
	15	200,000
	16	60,000
Total Estimated Paid Attendance:		**5,145,000**

The above-estimated attendance, which for several reasons may be itself optimistic, is over 1.6 million less than the 6.8 million ticket sales being boldly predicted. This would translate to a financial shortfall of more than $63 million. One need be neither bean counter nor doubting Thomas to suggest that the financial picture for the Atlanta Games seems unsettling. There presently appears to be a real potential for a shortfall of at least $111 million ($48M + $63M) in Olympic revenues. The figure could go higher.

The author readily admits that the above figures, which are thought to be rational but hardly authoritative, do not agree with the opinions of experts that the Atlanta Olympics are headed for a break-even success at the very least. My figures are based on obviously incomplete information. Still, the information that is available raises an abundance of caution flags. It may be that, as the Olympic picture is clarified, all causes for present questioning will evaporate. It is also possible that alarm bells will sound.

The Atlanta Games will do well indeed if they can approximate the financial success of the 1984 Olympics in Los Angeles. Atlanta organizers reportedly have raised almost twice as much as the total revenues in the Los Angeles Games. But the Atlanta Games' budget is more than three times larger than the 1984 budget.

The zone between optimism and candor is an interesting one. It was never approached by observers of preparations for the 1976 Montreal Olympics, the most financially disastrous in history. Just a few months prior to those Games, observers said of Montreal: "The enthusiasm and energy that the members of the organising committee have put and are putting into the Games is a guarantee of their success."

Hard work and enthusiasm obviously are not a sure prescription. Neither is pessimism especially helpful. The middle ground for now seems to recommend wariness.

BUBBA THE BLUE SLUG, NOBEL LAUREATES AND MUCH MORE

Atlanta's Olympic mascot has been coddled, criticized and laughed at. It was at first called Whatizit. Most Atlantans said they did not know. Although no more improbable than many of the cartoon chickens and goofy gargoyles that parade as mascots in sports at large, the Olympics' creature in Atlanta has not been popular, at least not with adults. The object of derision is referred to as a sperm with legs, Bubba the Blue Slug, or simply "the Olympic mascot from hell". The name Izzy now is officially assigned. **Iffy** might be more fitting.

Some see the Georgia legislature as a rich source for cartoon characters, but the legislators in 1994 passed a law designed to help visitors to the Atlanta Games. The law requires that hotels during the Olympics must price rooms at 1994 rates with only a cost-of-living increase. In theory, a room that rented for $100 in 1994 should cost about $106 during the 1996 Games. In practice, hotels and others are busily looking for loopholes, trap doors, and pet legislators to change the law.

Controversy, that aging but undying companion to the Olympics, has set up shop in Atlanta. Maybe a mall. The original volleyball venue was spiked. It had been set for Cobb County in the northern Atlanta suburbs. But when Cobb commissioners passed a resolution condemning a "gay lifestyle", storms of protest arose within Atlanta's homosexual and feminist communities. Activists demanded that Cobb be stripped of the volleyball venue. The commissioners refused in 1994 to strike down the resolution. That was taken as the "seminal moment" according to one Olympic executive. The venue was transferred to Athens, Georgia, where it was gayly accepted for its $10 million economic impact.

The Georgia state flag controversy threatens to spill over into the Games. The Confederate battle emblem has been part of the state flag for some 40 years. It was put there as an assertion of states' rights in the uproar caused by Supreme Court rulings. Many blacks now want the emblem removed. They see it as an assault on human dignity. The other side claims that it is a memorial to valorous conduct in the Lost Cause and that in any event there is no reason to change the flag. Heated rhetoric on the state flag issue may flow during the Games,

Heated rhetoric on the state flag issue may flow during the Games, the third day of which happens to be the 135th anniversary of the first battle of Bull Run.

the third day of which happens to be the 135th anniversary of the first battle of Bull Run. Then again, it may be so hot around the mythic environs of Tara that no one will care.

There apparently are millions in America who care little at this point about the Olympics. An April 1995 poll by the *Atlanta Journal - Constitution* newspaper revealed that 40% of southerners and 51% of other Americans are unaware that Atlanta is to host the Games.

Yet the Olympics already preoccupy a wide segment of Atlanta's nearly three million people. Olympic construction is everywhere on the rise. A Los Angeles TV producer has been hired to put on the show for the Olympic opening and closing ceremonies. He produced Michael Jackson's 1994 Super Bowl half-time show, which is taken as a credit by the majority. The Olympic ceremonies, however, probably will be protected from "gangster rap".

The streets outside the Olympic venues may be less safe. Security in Atlanta promises to be heavy but no large American city is without crime. One thing is certain: it will not be Lillehammer. Or even Barcelona. Many will be holding their breath as the first-ever Olympics in America's Bible Belt intersects what seems a growing militancy from extremists within the religious right. Will the Olympic emphasis on peace and international friendship be misconstrued, or otherwise seized upon, by those intent on venting hostility against the "new world order"?

Then too, there is Atlanta's newfound (and unwanted) status. Atlanta was rated the most dangerous city in America by a 1995 book predictably entitled *City Crime Rankings*. The rankings were said to be derived from current FBI crime statistics. Atlanta's mayor Bill Campbell dismissed it all as a mere effort "to sell a book". This cannot be taken as a compelling refutation.

The Cultural Olympiad already is underway in Atlanta. It will culminate during the summer of 1996. This little understood adjunct of the Olympics has distant origins. The ancient Games awarded prizes not only to athletes but also for poetry, music and performances. The most successful Olympian of all time was Herodoros of Megara. He won the trumpeters' competition in ten successive Olympiads from 328-292 B.C., an incredible Olympic

Once called the Empire City of the South,
Atlanta's promoters now refer to it as the International City.

reign of four decades.

Atlanta's Cultural Olympiad emphasizes American artistic achievements and especially those of the South. But a recent segment dealt also with world literature. It featured eight Nobel laureates in literature. They conferred at the Carter Center in Atlanta. One suspects that this was no accident. The former president is pursuing the Nobel Peace Prize with the same doggedness that won him election to the state senate from southwest Georgia 30 years ago. He is doing all that the budget of the Carter Center will allow in pursuing this objective. It is his most protracted political campaign.

Those familiar with the above background, therefore, were not surprised when Wole Soyinka, a Nigerian playwright, spoke up in conference, and on tangent, to say, "I think we should ask all the warring factions of the world to return to the tradition of the Olympics where there was a universal truce during the Olympic Games." He then turned to fellow laureates for their reaction. There being no motion for censure, Mexico's Octavio Paz responded, "It is no doubt that we agree."

One laureate though was not entirely agreeable during his stay in Atlanta. Joseph Brodsky, the Russian-American poet, ventured that the hosting of the prestigious event was only to "increase [Atlanta's] position on the map". He further stated that, if the Olympics are serious about the arts, the laureates' books should be sold in Olympic venues. Three of the literary laureates were invited to read from their works during the Cultural Olympiad program. Brodsky was not one of them.

The chapter to this point has dealt little with the sports aspect of the Atlanta Games. One reason of course is that the individual competitors have yet to be determined. Remember the Dave-and-Dan decathlon contest that never happened? Yet sports as always will be at the center of the Games. Some will be official for the first time. New in Atlanta will be beach volleyball for men and women, softball and soccer for women, and mountain cycling for men and women.

Prophecy in sport is roulette.

Prophecy in sport is roulette. Nevertheless, a few Olympic guideposts are set here briefly for the Atlanta Games.

Athletes to watch. In gymnastics, ***Vitaly Scherbo*** of Belarus could return to become the top gold-medal winner in the history of the Modern Olympics. He needs four which is within range for a superstar who won six in Barcelona. Look for ***Dan O'Brien***, or less likely ***Dave Johnson***, to return in the decathlon with something to prove. As in 1992, Texaco may want to fill O'Brien's tank.

Sports to watch. One old and one new. The ***men's soccer*** championship could go to a South American team for the first time in 68 years. Hotlanta has no shoreline but scantily clad Olympians making acrobatic saves in ***beach volleyball*** may prove to be a winner with spectators in the heat and in the Games as they have come to be: recreation raised to sport. Californians will find that Jonesboro's "Atlanta Beach" is not Malibu.

Countries to watch. With no Unified Team to spoil the party, the ***United States*** can become the leader in most medals by country, in Games unmarred by boycott, for the first time since 1968. ***Germany*** will be glad to take the head place at the medals table, for the first time in 60 years, if the United States falters.

China could start collecting Olympic medals in numbers more proportionate to its population, a billion people.

See the **Appendix** for the Atlanta Olympics' sports and venues and also for brief directions on venue locations.

The republics of the former Soviet Union, taken singly, are not the Olympic force of old. But Russia, Belarus and the Ukraine will field potent Olympic teams and will be competitive in almost every venue. Each will take home a load of medals and at least two of the three should finish among the top-ten countries by medals count.

Recall that Unified Team members got $3000 for every gold medal won in Barcelona. They were underpaid by new U.S. standards. Under the so-called Operation Gold program, American athletes now get $15,000 for every gold medal. Silver and bronze fetch $10,000 and $7500 each. The national push for Olympic medals is in overdrive. But in which direction is it taking us?

THE WINTER GAMES

*I was born with a chronic anxiety
about the weather.*
John Burroughs

There is always room at the top.
Daniel Webster

Chapter 8

QUEST FOR SOFT POWDER AND HARD GOLD

The Winter Games have been called a black sheep in the Olympic Movement. This is a strange tag for a festival bound in the whiteness of snow and ice. But Coubertin did not warm to the idea of a Winter Olympics because he thought, quite rightly, that it would favor a limited number of countries, namely those with mountains and cold climate. Avery Brundage, the I.O.C.'s president for 20 years, saw the Winter Games as promotion of professionalism and commercialization. He objected, for example, that salaried ski instructors competed as amateurs and that Olympic ski equipment prominently displayed the manufacturer's name.

But the Winter Olympics, once rooted, have never looked back. They enjoy vast popularity with audiences and have produced some of the best-known Olympic champions. Dorothy Hamill, the 1976 figure skating gold medalist, projected electricity on the ice and also introduced to millions of young women a new hair style, the "Hamill" wedge cut. It is difficult to imagine such a wave, or wedge, of popular appeal coming out of track and field, although the latter are closely followed in the Olympics. The most watched of Olympic events on television, and perennially near the top of all TV sports in ratings, are the women's figure skating finals.

Yet it is true that the Winter Olympics favor a limited number of nations. Zaire is unlikely to be well represented, though the Jamaican bobsled team, as a novelty, has received ample TV coverage in recent Games.

The mountainous countries of Europe have dominated all 17 of the Winter Olympics to date with one exception. The United States led in the medals count in 1932 when the Games were tucked away in Lake Placid, New York, and were skipped by many of Europe's best winter athletes. Otherwise, Norway and the former Soviet Union have been especially successful in their quest for hard gold in the soft powder of the Winter Olympics. Each has led in gold medals on seven occasions. Norway's triumph in 1948 was shared with Sweden and Switzerland. Germans won the most championships in 1984 and 1992. With reunification of East and West Germany since 1990, Germany appears destined to be high in the medals standings for the foreseeable future.

The Winter Games are not large by Summer Games' standards. See the **Appendix** (A.6) for participation figures. Less than 2000 athletes showed up for the 1994 Games in Lillehammer, Norway, while Atlanta expects some 10,000 athletes. Lillehammer was host to 67 countries. Atlanta plans for almost 200. The Winter Olympics feature only seven sports but the summer list has grown to 25.

The Modern Olympics have been criticized for not being inclusive enough and in particular for not promoting sports which are accessible to countries in the Third World. To the extent that the Olympics become more inclusive, it will probably occur in the Summer Games. The well-tooled Japanese and Koreans, hardly third-world nations, are making inroads in Olympic winter sports. However, the island of Seychelles, an I.O.C. member in the Indian Ocean, is unlikely to field an ice hockey team. The reasons are manifest and include the fact that an ice rink can be many hundreds of times more expensive to construct than, say, a row of badminton courts or a soccer field.

The quest though for Olympic gold in snowy venues is keen — when they are snowy. That brings us to another problem. The weather. It can be problematical even in normally cold climates. Over a third of all Winter Olympics have been plagued with marginal weather or worse. The Games of 1924, 1928, 1932, 1964, 1968 and 1972 experienced weather problems ranging from rain and thaw to blizzard and gale. Fortunately, Olympic organizers for the most part have been able to improvise solutions. The Austrian Army hauled in almost 20,000 cubic meters of snow for the 1964 Olympics in Innsbruck. That is enough snow to cover an entire football field to a depth of nearly four feet. What made the operation especially nightmarish was that this immense volume had to be hauled up mountains over 8000 feet high.

The Winter Games have not been easy. Yet ease has never been an Olympic trademark. The Winter Games have worked because the mountains that present the barrier also pose the challenge and the spectacle.

The Winter Games have worked because the mountains that present the barrier also pose the challenge and the spectacle.

THE SNOWS OF YESTERYEAR AND HOT ITEMS, 1924-1984

Figure skating was a demonstration sport in the London Olympics in 1908. The men's champion was Sweden's Ulrich Salchow, who originated the single-revolution jump which bears his name. Ice hockey and figure skating were demonstration sports in the 1920 Olympics at Antwerp. It was not until 1924 that the Winter Olympics were established as a separate festival.

The 1920 Games saw the first Olympic appearance of Gillis Grafstrom of Sweden, the only man ever to win three crowns in figure skating. Upon breaking a skate at Antwerp, he simply went to town and purchased an old-fashioned, curly-toed one. Grafstrom tried for a fourth successive gold medal in the 1932 Winter Olympics at Lake Placid, New York, but came second after an accidental collision with a photographer on the ice. Afterward, the winner in men's figure skating, Karl Schafer of Austria, said, "Yes, I beat him, but he is still the world's greatest skater."

Sonja Henie of Norway was the world's greatest woman skater for more than a decade. She participated at age 11 in the inaugural Winter Games of 1924 in Chamonix, France. She was last among eight competitors. But the child developed grown-up work habits including a seven-hour daily training regimen. She never lost in competition after age 13. Henie won ten consecutive world championships in women's figure skating. She was the gold medalist in three successive Olympics from 1928 through 1936. Her repertoire included a whirl with up to 80 spins.

Henie was the first in a long procession of famous Olympic

skaters to go on to lucrative appearances as part of the Ice Capades. She also was a rarity among Olympians pursuing film careers. Hugely successful, she earned a million dollars in 1939 and was the number three box office attraction in America, behind Shirley Temple and Clark Gable. It was accurately said of Henie, however, that "her acting was on a par with Charles Laughton's figure skating."

Except for appearances by Sonja Henie, the Winter Games of

Sonja Henie at 23 received her third successive
Olympic gold medal and interested looks from several Nazis.

1928 in St. Moritz, Switzerland, and those in 1932 at Lake Placid were in many ways not distinguished. However, one American athlete at Lake Placid did something which established him as unique in Olympic annals. Eddie Eagan won a gold medal in the four-man bobsled event. Eagan had won the Olympic light heavyweight boxing crown 12 years earlier in Antwerp. He is the only person to date ever to win gold medals in both the Winter and Summer Games.

The 1936 Games in Garmisch-Partenkirchen, Germany, saw a splendid performance by a Norwegian speed skater. Ivar Ballangrud won the 500, 5000 and 10,000-meter races and took the silver medal in the 1500-meter event.

Sapporo, Japan, was scheduled to host the 1940 Winter Olympics but withdrew because of the Sino-Japanese War. Garmisch-Partenkirchen agreed in June 1939 to repeat as host city but within three months all was cancelled due to the outbreak of the Second World War.

After the war, America's Richard Button burst upon the Winter

Olympic scene. The only gold medalist in skating ever to attend Harvard Law School, Button won the men's Olympic figure skating championship in 1948 at St. Moritz and in 1952 at Oslo. In St. Moritz, he became the first skater in Olympic competition ever to do a flawless double axel (three turns in the air). The high-jumping Button in the 1952 Games was the first to perform a successful triple-loop jump. It was fact not mere boast when he said, "I can't copy anyone else because nobody has anything new."

Not everyone at the Oslo Games was as athletic as Button. Two German winners were very much in the hole with regard to fitness. The two-man bobsled champions together weighed over 520 pounds and looked more like winners of a pizza-eating contest than Olympic gold medalists. Some Olympic torsos need more than Myron.

The 1956 Winter Olympics in Cortina d'Ampezzo, Italy, with reason have been called Toni Sailer's Games. The Austrian superstar skier won all three Alpine events (downhill, slalom and giant slalom) for the first time in Olympic history. This feat has been matched only by France's Jean-Claude Killy in the 1968 Games.

The difference was that Sailer's victories were by impressive margins while those of Killy were close and marked by controversy. Yet such footnotes cause little pause. Both achievements are printed in the record book as bona fide Olympic sweeps. If stout victories grow thin in the course of time, footnotes on victories virtually disappear. This book carries but one footnote in its text, a minimal reference to the past greatness of the Circus Maximus.

Squaw Valley, California, hosted the 1960 Winter Games. Only a tourist hostel stood there when the remote site, 200 miles east of San Francisco, was selected by the I.O.C. But Soviet speed skater Lydia Skoblikova was to stand there and to prevail. The Siberian school teacher won the 1500 and 3000-meter races, the former in world-record time. She towered even more in the 1964 Games where she came first in the events at 500, 1000, 1500 and 3000 meters. She won the first three of her four gold medals in 1964 with Olympic-record times, the most dazzling display of speed and power in ice skating prior to Eric Heiden's phenome-

Speed skater Lydia Skoblikova leads all Winter Olympic champions with six gold medals.

nal sweep of five events in 1980. Skoblikova was in the camera's eye at Squaw Valley, where the first TV rights for an Olympics were purchased by CBS for only $50,000.

The 1964 Games in Innsbruck, Austria, were to the Winter Olympics what the 1936 Big Show in Berlin had been to the Summer Games. It was a new summit even if the summit lacked snow. The weather at Innsbruck was the mildest in almost 60 years. Snow was trucked in as part of the most desperate campaign by Austrian soldiers since the First World War. The mountainsides were heroically readied. Over a million spectators watched nearly 1200 athletes in competition. The Winter Games for the first time were fully computerized. The first great figure skating pairs from the Soviet Union, the incomparable Protopopovs, made their debut and quickly raised the event to new heights with their timeless elegance and spellbinding "death spiral". Ludmila Belousova and Oleg Protopopov won in Innsbruck and repeated as gold medalists, at ages 32 and 35, in the 1968 Grenoble Games.

The most timeless act at Innsbruck, however, belonged to a bobsled participant in the twilight of his career. Eugenio Monti of Italy, many times a world champion but never an Olympic one, scuttled his chances in the two-man bobsled event when he came to the rescue of Britain's Tony Nash, who was about to lose his run for a medal because of a sheared bolt. Monti volunteered a bolt from his bobsled and Nash went on to win the gold medal.

But the steep slopes of competition sometimes lead to a happy ending. In the Grenoble Games four years later, Monti at age 40 won a gold medal in the four-man bobsled. Good guys do not always finish last though they never finish younger. The feat is timeless but the feet are not.

Good guys do not always finish last though they never finish younger. The feat is timeless but the feet are not.

The shadow of time obviously was on Jean-Claude Killy's mind in Grenoble. The hero of the 1968 Games retired saying, "It is my firm belief that an athlete should retire from sports at the climax of his career." Few would argue that Killy's Alpine sweep was anything other than a fitting climax. To date it has never been repeated in the Olympics. Speaking of climaxes, women competitors at Grenoble were asked for the first time in Olympic history to submit to a sex test.

The 1972 Winter Olympics went to Sapporo 32 years behind schedule. The wait bore singular fruit for the Japanese. Yukio Kasaya won the gold medal in the normal hill event at 70 meters to become the only non-European ever to win an Olympic ski-jumping championship. But the wait for Austrian skier Karl Schranz was a short one. He was expelled at the outset of the Games for permitting the use of his name and picture in advertising.

Will Grimsley, sports editor of the Associated Press, argued that the expulsion was unfair and that such an approach ultimately restricts the Olympics as a preserve of the rich: "This thing of amateur purity is something that dates back to the nineteenth century when amateur sportsmen were regarded as gentlemen and everyone else was an outcast. The Olympics should be a competition of skill and strength and speed — and no more."

The 1976 Winter Games returned to Innsbruck. Denver, Colorado, initially was selected as the host city but withdrew when the state government refused to guarantee financial support. At Innsbruck, Ulrich Wehling of East Germany returned and won a second consecutive gold medal in the Nordic combined, an event comprised of ski jumping and cross-country skiing. Wehling won the Nordic championship again in 1980 to become the only skier ever to win three successive gold medals in the Olympics.

Wehling's career ran parallel to that of Russia's Irina Rodnina, perhaps the greatest pairs figure skater in Olympic history. She teamed with Aleksei Ulanov to win the gold medal in 1972. She won two more gold medals skating with Aleksandr Zaitsev in 1976 and 1980. Rodnina is a major star in what may be the Winter Olympics' most heralded constellation, the figure skating venue. Certainly, the most impressive reign in the Winter Games is that of the pairs figure skaters of the former Soviet Union, who have ruled the event since 1964, more than 30 years.

The dominance of the Russian ice hockey team has been almost as remarkable. The Russians have fallen short of winning the gold medal in ice hockey only twice in the Winter Games since 1956. On both occasions, 1960 and 1980, the team crown was won by the United States on an American ice rink. The dramatic victory by Team USA in 1980 is among the most frequently recollected Olympic vignettes from the archives of American television.

The highest achievement by an individual in the history of the Winter Games is that of America's Eric Heiden. He skated with-

TONY DUFFY/ALLSPORT

Speed skater Eric Heiden in 1980 turned in the kind of Olympic performance that with luck one expects to see a few times in a given century.

out effect in the 1976 Innsbruck Games, but in 1980 at Lake Placid he turned in one of the most astounding Olympic performances of any season. Heiden swept all five speed skating events in record times. He broke the Olympic records at 500, 1000, 1500 and 5000 meters. He broke the world record at 10,000 meters. Heiden won everything there was to win with speed skates on the ice. It is difficult to do more in sports than what was done. It is difficult to explain in words what was done. At some point, superlatives fail and the achievement itself is wholly articulate.

UNDER SEIGE: A CITY, HEARTS, KNEES AND RECORDS, 1984-1994

Sarajevo, Yugoslavia, was host to the 1984 Winter Olympics. But the city's name today conjures up thoughts of war and destruction instead of peace and friendship. The war in what was Yugoslavia has raged for much of the time since the Sarajevo Games. Hundreds of thousands of people have been killed or injured. Sarajevo itself for several years has been under seige. It now stands, largely in ruin, as a stark reminder of the Olympic dream unfulfilled.

The winter of 1984 was a happier time for Sarajevo — and for American athletes. Two U.S. skiers became the only non-Europeans ever to win Olympic gold medals in men's Alpine events. Bill Johnson won the downhill championship and Phil Mahre took the crown in the slalom.

Hearts were under seige in Sarajevo's figure skating venue. An East German beauty, Katarina Witt, won the women's figure skating championship. After the Olympic victory, she received 35,000 love letters from those smitten in front of their TV sets. The success and seduction continued in the 1988 Winter Games in Calgary, Canada, where Witt became the only woman since Sonja Henie to win a successive individual gold medal in figure skating. Both Witt and America's Debbie Thomas in their programs skated to the music of Bizet's *Carmen*. Witt had the erotic looks attributed to Carmen while Thomas, also attractive, had Carmen's bad luck. It was all over when Thomas, who was last to skate, missed a triple toe loop early in her performance.

Witt participated in the 1994 Games as a professional but placed only seventh. Yet her seal and spell on the sport will not soon fade. She was wise to the ways of axels and men. "I rather think every man prefers looking at a well-built woman," she ventured. Few question her expertise.

The 1988 Calgary Games saw the debut of Bonnie Blair, the greatest U.S. woman athlete in Olympic winter sport. She won the 500-meter championship in speed skating in Calgary. Blair, in 1992 and again in the accelerated 1994 Games, won at 500 and 1000 meters. Her record of five gold medals exceeds that of any other U.S. female athlete in Winter or Summer Olympics, though some might argue that Blair was assisted by the fact that her last two Games were only two years apart. This acceleration will be discussed shortly. In any event, only Lydia Skoblikova and the Unified Team's Lyubova Egorova have won more gold medals (six each) than Blair in the Winter Games.

NATIONAL OLYMPIC COMMITTEE OF GERMANY

Twice Olympic figure skating champion Katarina Witt combined eroticism and athleticism.

American women have performed somewhat better than U.S. men in recent Winter Games. "We [women] don't have professional football, baseball or basketball," Blair explains. "For us, the Olympics are the highest you can get in athletic achievement." It might also be added that in Europe, more so than in the United States, many of the best male athletes gravitate toward winter sports.

The 1992 Winter Olympics in Albertville, France, were directed in part by Jean-Claude Killy, the French hero of the 1968 Games. Just three hours before the opening ceremony at Albertville, the 17-member team from war-ravaged Bosnia-Herzegovina arrived from the beseiged capital of Sarajevo.

The Italian skier Alberto Tomba predicted that the 1992 Games would be the "Alberto-ville" Olympics. But this was not to be. The Italian playboy, who won the Alpine slalom and giant events in 1988, defended only the latter successfully in 1992.

The top athlete at Albertville was a woman cross-country skier, Lyubova Egorova of the Unified Team. She won three gold and two silver medals, including individual championships at 10 and 15 kilometers. Egorova went on to win three gold medals and a silver in the 1994 Games in Lillehammer, where her cross-country victories included individual crowns in the 5-kilometer classical and 10-kilometer pursuit races. The Siberian athlete established a record for top medals (6-3-0) without equal in the Winter Olympics.

Another woman cross-country skier from the former Soviet Union has a credible claim as one of the all-time best women in winter sport. Raisa Smetanina competed in five successive Winter Games, a record in itself, from 1976 through 1992. She won individual gold medals in cross-country races at 10 kilometers in 1976 and at 5 kilometers in 1980. Smetanina during her venerable Olympic career won a total of 10 medals (4-5-1), more than any other person in the history of the Winter Olympics.

The Games in Lillehammer, Norway, were accelerated. The I.O.C. in 1988 decided that, beginning at Lillehammer in 1994, the Winter and Summer Games would be separated, thus staging an Olympics every two years. The Games to follow Lillehammer are the 1996 Summer Olympics in Atlanta. The 1998 Winter Olympics will be held in Nagano, Japan, and the Summer Games in 2000 will be in Sydney, Australia. Salt Lake City will host the Winter Games of 2002.

The decision to alter the Olympic schedule is part of the Samaranch legacy. It is motivated chiefly by economics and justified by simple calculation. More pie will be eaten, and therefore crucially more pie sold, in marathon 16-day sessions separated by distance of two years than in the same sessions separated by only a few months. The separation reduces the risk of saturation and it increases advertising opportunities. The Olympics become a kind of new-age movable feast. The staggered schedule is also less taxing on Olympic committee staffs.

The Winter Games in Lillehammer were only the second to be held in Norway. The prior Games were in Oslo in 1952. Norway has an illustrious Winter Olympic history but had not come first at the medals table in over a quarter of a century. Norway reestablished its winning ways at Lillehammer by taking 26 medals (10-11-5). The United States was fifth, not a surprising placement, with 13 medals (6-5-2).

Bjorn Dahlie, Norway's best cross-country skier in Olympic history, won individual gold medals in the 10-kilometer classical and 15-kilometer pursuit events. He won individual Olympic crowns in the 1992 Games at distances of 15 and 50 kilometers. Dahlie is Norway's all-time top Olympian by medals count (5-3-0).

Another Norwegian, however, gave the most spectacular performance at Lillehammer. Johann Koss won gold medals at 1500, 5000 and 10,000 meters in speed skating. The operative word is *speed*. Koss won all three races in world-record times, thereby asserting and justifying his nickname, the Boss. He retired from Olympic competition with four gold medals and a silver, won in the 1992 and 1994 Games, in order to attend medical school.

Koss' three world records at Lillehammer equalled the number of world records established in all of track and field, mens' and womens' events, in the 1992 Summer Games. While world records are proving more difficult in certain summer sports, Winter Olympic athletes seem to be still sharpening their blades — and sights.

American figure skater Nancy Kerrigan fell within the sights of an assailant. Five weeks prior to the Lillehammer Games, Kerrigan while at practice was hammered on the right knee with a metal baton. The injury was serious but Kerrigan recovered through pluck and therapy. The assailant was later captured and convicted. His criminal act apparently was requested by the husband of another American figure skater, Tonja Harding. It became clear also that Harding had at least some knowledge that the attack was to occur and that its intent was to eliminate Kerrigan as a contender for an Olympic medal. Kerrigan and Harding studiedly avoided each other at Lillehammer.

In an exceptionally close finals, 16-year-old Oksana Baiul of the Unified Team won the women's figure skating gold medal. She was the youngest champion since Sonja Henie. Baiul is an orphan. Her countenance indeed was a charming mixture of waif, pixy and emerging swan. She too had to overcome an injury, one caused by a collision in practice on the ice the day before the final competition. Baiul needed a pain-killing injection in order to compete. Her program was inspired perfection. Kerrigan, who also skated to near perfection, came second.

Tonja Harding interrupted her final program shortly after it began and pleaded to the judges, with strained gestures, that she had not been given enough time to tie her shoelaces. Allowed to restart, she stooped low to secure her laces but not as low as in prior acts against Kerrigan. Harding, a pre-Olympics favorite, placed eighth.

The figure skating pairs championship in 1994 was won by Ekaterina Gordeeva and Sergei Grinkov, the gold medalists in 1988 as well. They returned, after marriage and starting a family, to win at Lillehammer over the brilliant 1992 champions, another Russian pair, who took the silver medal. Seldom has ice been graced, in the words of the poet, with such bodies "swayed to music" and "brightening glance".

South Korea dominated the short-track speed skating events for both men and women. This could be a significant development. It seems to be the first real fracture in the strangle hold that Europeans, and to a much lesser extent Americans, have enjoyed in events during the 70-year history of the Winter Olympics.

The 1994 Games marked the tenth anniversary of those in Sarajevo. Nine athletes represented Bosnia-Herzegovina. In the clean quietness of Lillehammer, many thoughts turned to the meaning of Sarajevo. Does the conflict there highlight the fragility of

The image of Sarajevo for many reasons is a reflection of the century's desperation and hope.

Sarajevo, host city to the 1984 Winter Games,
is at war and under seige.

Olympic ideals worthy of preservation or does it strip down pretenses which in any event are not sustainable?

The agony of Sarajevo suggests both the limits and persistence of the Olympic spirit. The city is captive in a nation at war and under seige. Yet athletes from that nation continue to participate in the Modern Olympic Games. It is both incongruous gesture and magnificent symbol. The image of Sarajevo for many reasons is a reflection of the century's desperation and hope.

THE ONCE AND FUTURE GREATS

*We see dimly in the Present
what is small and what is great.*
James Lowell

*Power when wielded by abnormal
energy is the most serious of facts.*
Henry Adams

Chapter 9

MARK SPITZ, WE HARDLY KNEW YE

This chapter makes an informed selection of the 11 greatest athletes in the history of the Modern Olympics. Why eleven? It would not be facetious to answer that I have avoided the commonplace identifier of Top Ten because the subjects are anything but commonplace. I have not named a dozen because I deal here with neither baked perishables nor disciples. Also, when I got to the twelfth name in this admittedly subjective listing, I felt perceptibly that the Olympic achievements of that athlete, though lofty, were not of the same order as the achievements of the preceding athletes. But the best answer for reaching 11 names can only be that of the observer on the ways of mystery, folly and the world: Why not?

Any discussion of all-time greats of the Modern Olympics carves in difficult rock. Some might question why the task even should be attempted or what it can accomplish. Are not there so many titans along this avenue that any choosing of higher giants is futile? Maybe. But the urge to make comparisons, whether of titans or mortals, is in our blood. In seeking to select that which seems best, we may glimpse, if imperfectly, that which is best in us.

The chapter will not apologize for the necessarily subjective nature of its selection. Nor will I deny that I have failed to include many athletes whose Olympic marks can only be approached with something akin to reverence. Any listing which omits the likes of Ray Ewry, Jim Thorpe, Jesse Owens, Sonja Henie, Sawao Kato and Matt Biondi, to name only a few, cannot confidently advertise itself as definitive.

The chapter does not advertise. It makes some informed

human judgments and arranges both fact and opinion with attempted brevity. The list avoids one of the most disturbing preoccupations of our time. Quotas. I have none. The hope throughout this brief discussion is that, where the list fails to attract agreement, it at least will attract attention to the subjects, whose athletic accomplishments are certainly among the most stirring of this or any century.

Whatever may be said about these 11 athletes, they form a highly contemporary listing. All of them are alive except Nurmi who died in 1973. Oerter, one of the elder statesmen, is not yet 60. These for the most part are young living legends. The Golden Age for modern Olympians is always apt to be in the recent memory and not because of public fickleness. I will proceed here generally in chronological order.

THE BEST OF THE BEST

Paavo Nurmi was the first Olympian of this century who might be called an international star. Athletes from the professional ranks such as heavyweight boxing champions Jack Johnson and Jack Dempsey attained wide fame before Nurmi. However, Nurmi was the first amateur athlete, using the term loosely but not indiscriminately as at present, to be interna-

Nurmi

tionally famous. With nine gold and three silver medals to his credit, he leads all male athletes who have ever participated in official Modern Olympic Games. He won seven individual gold medals. Nurmi was criticized for being mechanical. He raced against trains as a youth in Abo, Finland, and he ran with a stopwatch in hand as an adult. Yet these schedules pointed the way to his greatness, irresistible momentum and a surge to the finish line as relentless as time. Nurmi was the Abo Express.

The Olympic decathlon champion has no peer in Athletics (track and field). **Bob Mathias** was the youngest athlete ever to win the Olympics' two-day torture test. It was not unlike winning the Indianapolis 500 in one's first spurt of serious driving. At age 17. After his draining victory in the 1948 Games, through some

Mathias

of the worst weather in Summer Olympic history, the young Mathias told his father, "never again, never again". He did not mean it. Mathias returned in 1952 and became the first of only two athletes to win a successive Olympic decathlon. In post-Olympic competition in 1952, he ran the 110-meter hurdles in 13.8 seconds, a mark bettered at that time by only nine men. None of whom was a multi-event wonder like Mathias. He forfeited his amateur status, and chances in the 1956 Games for an unheard of third gold medal in the decathlon, by appearing in a 1953 film about his career. He was then all of 23. Mathias was never beaten in the decathlon. He remains today, for many, the unbeaten champion of Olympic champions.

Larissa Latynina set the meticulous standards by which we now evaluate women's gymnastics. She was the purist's purist. She won 18 Olympic medals, more than any other modern athlete. No one in official Games has won more gold medals than her nine, six of which were individual championships. She also won five silver and four bronze medals. Latynina was the first of only two women to win the all-around title in gymnastics in successive Games,

Latynina

1956 and 1960. Vera Caslavska took the all-around title in 1964 and 1968. Latynina ruled in floor exercise but, from 1956 through 1964, her reign too in women's gymnastics extended to the highest rafters.

Ask for the names of athletes winning individual gold medals in successive Olympics and a list of a few dozen remarkably gifted athletes can be compiled. Ask for those prevailing individually in three consecutive Games and the list is reduced to a handful of sports immortals. But ask for individual champions in four successive Modern Olympics and the response is singular. **Al Oerter**. He set Olympic records in the discus with each of his four victories, 1956 through 1968. Suffering a

Oerter

rib injury and with his right side heavily taped and packed in ice to prevent internal hemorrhage, Oerter won his third Olympic title in the discus in 1964. Nor did a rain-swamped throwing circle stop him from the historic fourth championship in the 1968 Games. He adjusted by eliminating his preliminary swings and made the three best throws of his entire career. "These are the Olympics," said Oerter. "You die for them." One got the impression that he was not just speaking figuratively. No Olympic athlete has demonstrated more strength in victory or more grittiness in adversity.

Aleksandr Medved is the greatest wrestler of the 20th century. He could also be the best in the past 2000 years. This may sound like hyperbole but one literally must go back more than two millennia and the time of the most renowned of ancient Greek athletes to find a wrestler of similar standing. Or takedown. Medved won the Olympic championship as a light heavyweight in 1964 and as a heavyweight in 1968. He was the first gold medalist in the new super heavy-

Medved

weight division in the 1972 Games. A nimble bear of a man, Medved was known for sudden attack and deft evasion. However, he rarely weighed more than his opponent. He won by speed, power and intelligence. He was the crafty Ulysses in a league of stalwart Ajaxes. Important to note is that Medved's Olympic victories came in an era of legendary wrestlers such as Turkey's Ahmet Ayuk and Wilfred Dietrich of Germany. Dietrich won five medals in freestyle and Greco-Roman wrestling in three Olympics. But he and others grappled in Medved's shadow. In addition to three Olympic gold medals, Medved won ten world championships in three weight divisions from 1962 through 1972. What Homer said of Ulysses' famous wrestling translates as well for the Ukrainian. Medved wrestled "with might" and "full of wiles" to take the prize.

Dial 9-1-1. Not for emergency but for Olympic greatness. That is the medals count for **Mark Spitz**, who leads all Americans in the Olympic medals category. Spitz, the definitive swimmer, made a historic splash in the 1972 Games. He took seven gold medals

Spitz

at Munich, the most ever won in a single Games. Four of the medals were in individual events and three in swimming relays. Spitz previously had won four medals in the 1968 Games: two golds for relays and a silver and a bronze for individual events. He won the Sullivan Award in 1971, the year *before* his spectacular triumph in Munich. The award is given annually by the Amateur Athletic Union to the athlete who "has done the most during the year to advance the cause of sportsmanship." The first recipient was Bobby Jones in 1930. Spitz was not in bad company. Neither are the athletes in this chapter who rise to the level of Spitz's enormous Olympic achievement. It is telling that Spitz's place is high but not dominant in their company. He and all others here stand among equals.

Teofilo Stevenson is to Modern Olympic boxing what Medved is to wrestling. Simply the best. Stevenson was easily the gold medalist as a super heavyweight in three Olympics. He won the title in 1972 in less than six rounds of boxing. The 1976 crown was his by way of a knockout. He won a convincing 4-1 decision to take the championship in the 1980 Games. Cuba boycotted the next two Olympics. Otherwise, Stevenson would have been the favorite to win

Stevenson

an unprecedented fourth gold medal in boxing in successive Games. He won all three amateur boxing world championships in which he entered, the last being in 1986. Few doubt that Stevenson, at 32, could have defeated Tyrell Biggs, the 1984 Olympic champion in the super heavyweight division. Stevenson emphatically chose never to turn professional. He doubtless passed up great personal wealth in this decision, along with wide sordidness in the wake of questionable promoters. Stevenson's Olympic predecessor was none other than George Foreman, untainted as the recent heavyweight professional champion and unchallenged in hamburger consumption. What professional path the younger, leaner and meaner Stevenson might have followed is a question which tantalizes the imagination. His name will not be recorded among the wealthy. But he probably will settle for being remembered as one of the century's greatest athletes.

Eric Heiden differs from the other ten Olympians in this listing in a couple of ways. He is the only representative for winter sports and he is the only athlete whose achievement rests on a single Games. Yet the enormity of Heiden's performance in the 1980 Winter Olympics sweeps away any doubt about his inclusion here. During a nine-day period at Lake Placid, the 21-year-old speed skater won every race that he entered, which is to say every speed skating event

Heiden

for men on the Olympic board. He set four Olympic records and one world record in the process. Heiden cut well over a second off the Olympic record at 500 meters, something not done for 24 years. He lowered the prior mark at 1000 meters by over four seconds, the greatest improvement ever in the short history of this event. He beat the old mark at 5000 meters by more than 22 seconds, the largest improvement in 20 years. And these performances were apart from his world record at 10,000 meters. However, as said previously of Heiden, the numbers only take us so far. It is enough to win all there is to win in one's Olympic sport and to do it in commanding fashion. No more is possible, even among the most mighty of Olympians.

It is enough to win all there is to win in one's Olympic sport and to do so in commanding fashion. No more is possible, even among the most mighty of Olympians.

The only man to date other than Bob Mathias to win the Modern Olympic decathlon twice is **Daley Thompson**. He was known for brash expressions of confidence. Yet he was able to put his mark where his mouth was. Thompson won the 1980 Games over two Russian rivals and in 1984 ahead of three Germans. The two Olympics were spoiled by major boycotts; but Thompson's performances were convincing, especially in 1984 when his victory set an Olympic decathlon record which still stands. He amassed 8798 points in Los Angeles, a world record at the time and one which fell only in 1992 to Dan O'Brien in post-

Thompson

Olympic competition. Robert Zmelik's decathlon victory in the 1992 Games was almost 200 points below the mark set by Thompson in Los Angeles. Few Olympic events are more volatile than the decathlon. Prior to Thompson's victory in Moscow, a new decathlon record was set in every Modern Olympics except three. Most of these were also world records. Thompson's 1984 record is the longest-standing for the decathlon in Olympic history.

The names of **Carl Lewis** and Jesse Owens are frequently associated. In the 1984 Games, Lewis duplicated Owens' stunning Olympic performance almost a half-century before by winning four gold medals in track and field. But the truth is that, great as was Owens, Lewis stands on a higher Olympic rung. He followed up the victories in Los Angeles with four more gold medals, two each in the Games of 1988 and 1992. Lewis has won more Olympic medals (8-1-1) in Athletics than any other American. Jesse Owens was voted by U.S. sports writers to be

Lewis

the best male athlete in track and field for the first half of the century. It might be argued that Nurmi at least had some claim to that title. In any event, the question arises, Who is likely to be chosen as the outstanding man of the century in Athletics? Carl Lewis' name will be high on almost every sports writer's short list.

But for a single second, **Jackie Joyner-Kersee** would be the only athlete in the Modern Olympics to win three successive multi-event championships. That was the margin by which she missed winning the Olympic heptathlon in 1984. Had she run the 800-meter event one second faster, she would have taken the gold medal. Instead, first place went to Australia's Glynis Nunn by a wafer-thin margin (6390 points to Joyner-Kersee's 6385). Joyner-Kersee left nothing to chance in the 1988 Games. She smashed the heptathlon world record with 7291 points. She also won the gold medal in the women's long jump with an Olympic record yet unbroken. She defended her

Joyner-Kersee

heptathlon crown in 1992 and added a silver medal in the long jump. Joyner-Kersee and Carl Lewis were the only athletes in track and field to win individual gold medals in both Seoul and Barcelona. She is to women's Athletics what he is for the men's category. Top of the line.

ENOUGH SUPERLATIVES

Although deserved, enough superlatives have been issued here to justify a summation that is simple and direct. See the **Appendix** (A.7) for a list of the astounding improvements in Summer Olympic records for men in Athletics and swimming during the past century. Many of the athletes discussed above contributed disproportionate shares in lowering these Olympic marks.

It is not surprising that the most improved events in track and field, the Marathon and discus respectively, came to modern life only in the 1896 Games. Field events are most improved overall due to advances with technique, as in the shot put, and equipment innovations, as in the pole vault where the bamboo pole was replaced by fiberglass. The 5000-meter race may be the least improved in track because the first Olympic champion in the event was none other than the original Flying Finn, Hannes Kolehmainen.

The under-two hour Marathon looms as the next great barrier in Athletics. A time in less than two hours would be an 8% improvement over the current Olympic record set in 1984. Runners have managed to lower the Olympic mark by only 4% during the past 35 years. No one doubts, however, that the barrier will fall — in this century or the next.

The 11 superstars discussed previously project in their careers the meaning of the Olympic motto, *Swifter, Higher, Stronger*. This is not merely a phrase for Olympic athletes. It is reality. The above Olympic greats won by speed, power, and above all commitment. The best of future Olympic champions will surely embody these same virtues.

Chapter 10

THE POWER OF THE OLYMPICS

The Olympics are "the longest lasting social activity that exists." They exercise power over, and in turn are powered by, nations, commerce and individuals. The Games even have influenced the way in which man looks to heaven. The Olympian festivals were the Games of God. We know as much of the gods through the first Games as we know of the Games through their gods. Dead Greeks all.

What is not dead is that the Games continue to matter. Nations have spent vast treasure and will spend more because the Modern Olympics are of consequence to them.

The official Olympic disclaimer urges that the Games are not a competition between nations. However, it is clear that countries vie for prestige and power through the Olympics. Hitler had the 1936 Games carefully choreographed as propaganda. Japan, Germany, Russia and South Korea, during the past 35 years, each spent billions of dollars to host Games specifically aimed at projecting powerful and progressive national images to the world. Every hosting nation is anxious to showcase its best.

The Soviets and East Germans developed sports programs highly proficient in mining Olympic gold. The United States and other countries pay athletes handsome bounties for winning Olympic medals. These national programs are not about the ascendant role of sports. They are about national enhancement.

The tally of Olympic standings by country draws international attention. It is not an official scoring but neither is it an academic exercise. The United States has led in Olympic medals count in almost half of the Summer Games to date. See the **Appendix** (A.3 and 4). The former Soviet Union dominated after entering

Olympic competition in 1952. The Soviets won 6 of 10 Summer Games by medals count through 1988. Their Unified Team came first at Barcelona in 1992.

Nations on the Pacific rim, especially China and South Korea, may well challenge European countries in the Olympic medals standing within coming decades. The prospective shift tells much and not merely about athletics.

The power of commerce in the Olympics has been frequently cited. Power is a neutral term. It is force. Whether it is for good or otherwise is initially undecided in the equation.

The Games are big business yet seldom show a profit. This is distinct from saying that companies do not make money from the Olympics. But as with certain corporations that are so large as to be seen as indispensable, the modern Games by history have enjoyed ultimate financial backing from the governments surrounding the host city.

The influence of the Olympics is seen most vividly in the lives of individuals. Athletes and spectators. For the athlete, the Games provide an opportunity for recognition, wealth and fulfillment. They are a chance to leave one's footprint, not for all time but for time enough.

The Olympics occasionally have exerted a power over athletes which became self-destructive. The pressure to win is so great that some athletes have turned to drugs to increase performance. These abuses have been especially evident in the Summer Games, in part because many of its sports, such as Athletics and weightlifting, emphasize explosive strength. The torrent of fallen world and Olympic records last seen in the 1972 Summer Games has not been repeated, due in large measure to tighter and more extensive drug testing in the Olympics.

For the spectator, the Games are entertainment and something more. They provide a stroll on increasingly rare real estate in the modern world, a level playing field. Affirmative action is a negative consideration in hurling the discus. "Sports hold a special place for billions of people because they represent competition among athletes striving for excellence under fair rules that have been openly agreed upon." The fan too may enjoy sports for the play of emotion and chance among the iron girders of ability and experience.

But the Olympics add something extra. Ritual. Our era has seen an indifference for many traditional forms and institutions. To withstand the test of time, in some views washed by modern acid, is to withstand the next half-hour. The pomp and circumstance of the Games since 1920 evoke a belief that such long-standing proceedings (75 years is a modern eternity) are important and worthy of preservation.

The Olympic rings are an untidy chain. The Games as ritual remind us that we are connected in a continuum which winds from the deeds of the once-vibrant dead into a future landscape that we can but faintly imagine.

The Games as ritual remind us that we are connected in a continuum which winds from the deeds of the once-vibrant dead into a future landscape that we can but faintly imagine.

However, the argument for ritual can be taken too far. The stamp of Michael Jackson and fellow travelers apparently has become at least as important in recent Olympic ceremonies as the release of white pigeons.

Future spectators probably will experience the Olympics at different levels. There may never be a complete substitute for a venue seat, but technologies now opening will influence how we see the Games of the future. Spectators, using "interactive" television, should be able to select the precise events in which they are interested. We are only in the first stages of determining how "virtual reality" could influence the way we explore hundreds of experiences, including the Olympics.

Unfortunately, virtual-reality possibilities promise little for enjoying the Olympics as a community experience. On the contrary, if the individual spectator is hooded and thereby isolated by technology, the Games lose much of their appeal as ritual and shared experience. Many people therefore may forgo technological offerings in order to visit certain experiences in traditional ways.

But we need not resort to high-tech images to determine where the Olympics are or where they can and cannot take us. The Games have produced athletic records and commercialization at a dizzying pace. They can bring nations together in peace and in a place of regulated (if often frenzied) competition. But they cannot insure a peace without. The Olympics can manage how we enjoy the peace but not whether we suffer war. The Games seem powerless to prevent the outrages which have plagued our century and which continue still in places like Sarajevo. They are powerless to protect even those who have shared the inner circles.

The modern Games cannot control but at their best they may achieve something more important. By one rung at a time, they can help to elevate and inspire the human spirit.

APPENDIX

A. 1

1996 SUMMER GAMES:
EVENTS AND SPORTS BY VENUE

Opening Ceremony, Olympic Stadium, July 19 (8:30 pm)

Closing Ceremony, Olympic Stadium, August 4 (9:00 pm)

VENUE	SPORT	DATES
ATLANTA		
Olympic Stadium	**Track & Field**	July 26-29,31 & August 1-3
World Congress Center	**Fencing**	July 20-25
	Team Handball	July 24 31 & August 1-3
	Judo	July 20-26
	Table Tennis	July 23-31 & August 1
	Weightlifting	July 20-30
	Wrestling	July 20-23, 30-31 and August 1-2
Georgia Tech Alexander Coliseum	**Boxing**	July 20-28,30-31 and August 1-4
Aquatic Center	**Diving**	July 26-31 and August 1-2
	Swimming	July 20-26
	Synchronized Swimming	July 30, August 2
Omni Coliseum	**Volleyball**	July 20-31 and August 1-4
Georgia Dome	**Basketball**	July 20-31 and August 1-4
	Artistic Gymnastics	July 20-25, 28-29
	Team Handball	August 4
Atlanta University Clark-Atlanta and Morris Brown	**Field Hockey**	July 20-31 and August 1-2
Morehouse	**Basketball**	July 20-25, 28-30
Georgia State University	**Badminton**	July 24-31 and August 1

| Atlanta-Fulton County Stadium | **Baseball** | July 20-25, 27-30 and August 1-2 |
| Wolf Creek Complex (East Point) | **Shooting** | July 20-27 |

Modern Pentathlon will be held at four locations (Wolf Creek, World Congress Center, Georgia Tech Aquatic Center and Conyers) on July 30.

Road Cycling wheels around Atlanta's Buckhead on July 21 and 31 and August 3. No ticket required.

OUTSIDE ATLANTA

Athens, Georgia	**Rhythmic Gymnastics**	August 1-4
	Soccer Finals	July 28,31 and August 1-3
	Volleyball	July 20-29
Stone Mountain, Georgia	**Archery**	July 29-31 and August 1-2
	Cycling (Velodrome)	July 24-28
	Tennis	July 23-31 and August 1-2
Conyers, Georgia	**Equestrian**	July 21-29, 31 and August 1&4
	Mountain Cycling	July 30
Gainesville, Georgia (Lake Lanier)	**Canoe/Kayak (Sprint)**	July 30-31 and August 1-4
	Rowing	July 21-28
Jonesboro, Georgia ("Atlanta Beach")	**Beach Volleyball**	July 23-28
Columbus, Georgia	**Women's Softball**	July 21-27, 29-30
Savannah, Georgia (Wassaw Sound)	**Yachting**	July 22-31 and August 1

OUTSIDE GEORGIA

Ducktown, Tennessee (Ocoee River)	**Canoe/Kayak (Slalom)**	July 26-28
Birmingham, Alabama	**Soccer**	July 20-25, 27-28
Miami, Florida	**Soccer**	July 20-25, 27-28
Orlando, Florida	**Soccer**	July 20-25
Washington, D.C.	**Soccer**	July 20-25

A. 2

VENUE LOCATIONS FOR 1996 SUMMER GAMES

ATLANTA

Olympic Stadium

About 1.5 miles south of **Five Points, the center of downtown Atlanta**; on Interstate Highway 75/85 a half mile south of the Interstate junction of 75/85 and 20.

World Congress Center

285 International Boulevard, NW; just over a 10-minute walk northwest from **Five Points**.

Georgia Tech Alexander Coliseum Aquatic Center

The campus of the Georgia Institute of Technology (Georgia Tech) is about 1.5 miles north of **Five Points**. The Alexander Coliseum is in the northeast corner of the campus and the Aquatic Center is on the west side of the campus.

Omni Coliseum

Immediately south of the **World Congress Center**, the **Omni** is a 10-minute walk northwest from **Five Points**.

Georgia Dome

Just over a 10-minute walk northwest from **Five Points**. The **Dome**, **Omni** and **World Congress Center** are clustered together.

Atlanta University

This predominantly black university center is about 1.5 miles southwest of **Five Points**. Clark-Atlanta and Morris Brown are on Martin Luther King Drive while Morehouse is at the intersection of Fair and Ashby Streets.

Georgia State University

A downtown university only a couple of hundred yards southeast of **Five Points**.

Atlanta-Fulton County Stadium

Immediately north of the **Olympic Stadium** and immediately south of the junction of Interstates 75/85 and 20.

Wolf Creek Complex

In southwest Fulton County about seven miles west of Atlanta's international airport; just over 20 miles, a half-hour drive, southwest from downtown.

OUTSIDE ATLANTA

Athens, Georgia

About 65 miles northeast of Atlanta (University of Georgia campus)

Stone Mountain, Georgia

Less than 20 miles east of Atlanta on U.S. Highway 78; about a 35-minute drive from downtown *(if traffic is light, which may hardly be the case for all venues in and around Atlanta during the Games)*.

Conyers, Georgia

Just over 30 miles southeast of Atlanta on Interstate 20; about 45 minutes from downtown.

Gainesville, Georgia (Lake Lanier)

About 60 miles northeast of Atlanta on Interstate 85 and the Gainesville turnoff (I-985); Lake Lanier is west of Gainesville.

Jonesboro, Georgia ("Atlanta Beach")

25 miles south of Atlanta by way of Interstate 75 or U.S. Hwy 19/41.

Columbus, Georgia

About 110 miles southwest of Atlanta on Interstates 85 and 185.

Savannah, Georgia (Wassaw Sound)

Almost 260 miles southeast of Atlanta on Interstates 75 and 16; then figure on at least an hour by road and boat out to the sound, which is southeast of Savannah.

OUTSIDE GEORGIA

Ducktown, Tennessee (Ocoee River)

Just over 120 miles (about two and a half hours) north of Atlanta; the venue is about 15 minutes west of Ducktown on U.S. Hwy 64.

Birmingham, Alabama

About 155 miles west of Atlanta; Legion Field.

Miami, Florida

785 miles south of Atlanta; Orange Bowl Stadium.

Orlando, Florida

450 miles south of Atlanta; Florida Citrus Bowl.

Washington, D.C.

Atlanta is about 650 miles southwest of the nation's capital; Robert F. Kennedy Memorial Stadium.

A. 3

THE SUMMER OLYMPIC GAMES

Year	Olympiad	Site	Nations	Leader in Medals
1896	I	Athens	13	Greece, 47 (10-19-18)
1900	II	Paris	22	France, 102 (29-41-32)
1904	III	St. Louis	12	USA, 246 (80-85-81)
1908	IV	London	22	Britain, 145 (56-50-39)
1912	V	Stockholm	27	Sweden, 65 (24-24-17)
1916	VI	(Cancelled, World War I)		
1920	VII	Antwerp	29	USA, 95 (41-27-27)
1924	VIII	Paris	45	USA, 99 (45-27-27)
1928	IX	Amsterdam	46	USA, 56 (22-18-16)
1932	X	Los Angeles	37	USA, 103 (41-32-30)
1936	XI	Berlin	49	Germany, 89 (33-26-30)
1940	XII	(Cancelled, World War II)		
1944	XIII	(Cancelled, World War II)		
1948	XIV	London	59	USA, 84 (38-27-19)
1952	XV	Helsinki	69	USA, 76 (40-19-17)
1956	XVI	Melbourne	67	USSR, 98 (37-29-32)
1960	XVII	Rome	84	USSR, 103 (43-29-31)
1964	XVIII	Tokyo	94	USA, 90 (36-26-28)
1968	XIX	Mexico City	113	USA, 107 (45-28-34)
1972	XX	Munich	122	USSR, 99 (50-27-22)
1976	XXI	Montreal	92	USSR, 125 (49-41-35)
1980	XXII	Moscow	81	USSR, 195 (80-69-46)
1984	XXIII	Los Angeles	140	USA, 174 (83-61-30)
1988	XXIV	Seoul	160	USSR, 132 (55-31-46)
1992	XXV	Barcelona	172	UT, 112 (45-38-29)*
1996	XXVI	Atlanta		
2000	XXVII	Sydney		

* With the dismantlement of the Soviet Union in 1991, its former
republics participated in the 1992 Games as the Unified Team.

A. 4

COUNTRIES LEADING IN MEDALS
(SUMMER OLYMPICS, 1896 - 1992)

Country	Gold	Silver	Bronze	Total	Number of Games with Top Medals
United States	781	600	522	1903	10
USSR/Unified Team	440	357	315	1112	7
Germany *	334	357	358	1049	1
Britain	169	215	215	599	1
France	148	166	175	489	1
Sweden	133	145	165	443	1

* *Includes medals for both East Germany and West Germany from 1968 through 1988. East Germany alone, with 409 medals (153-129-127) in only five Summer Olympics, rose to rank just ahead of Sweden under a traditional scoring system which awards five points for a gold medal, three for silver and one for bronze.*

A. 5

THE WINTER OLYMPIC GAMES

Year	Winter Olympiad	Site	Nations	Leader in Top Medals
1924	I	Chamonix, France	16	Norway, 17 (4-7-6)
1928	II	St. Moritz, Switzerland	25	Norway, 15 (6-4-5)
1932	III	Lake Placid, New York	17	USA, 12 (6-4-2)
1936	IV	Garmisch-Partenkirchen, Germany	28	Norway, 15 (7-5-3)

(1940 and 1944 Games Cancelled, World War II)

Year	Winter Olympiad	Site	Nations	Leader in Top Medals
1948	V	St. Moritz, Switzerland	28	Norway & Sweden, 10 (4-3-3)
1952	VI	Oslo, Norway	30	Norway, 16 (7-3-6)
1956	VII	Cortina d'Ampezzo, Italy	32	USSR, 16 (7-3-6)
1960	VIII	Squaw Valley, California	30	USSR, 21 (7-5-9)
1964	IX	Innsbruck, Austria	36	USSR, 25 (11-8-6)
1968	X	Grenoble, France	37	Norway, 14 (6-6-2)
1972	XI	Sapporo, Japan	35	USSR, 16 (8-5-3)
1976	XII	Innsbruck, Austria	37	USSR, 27(13-6-8)
1980	XIII	Lake Placid, New York	37	USSR, 22 (10-6-6)
1984	XIV	Sarajevo, Yugoslavia	49	East Germany, 24 (9-9-6)
1988	XV	Calgary, Canada	57	USSR, 29 (11-9-9)
1992	XVI	Albertville, France	64	Germany, 26(10-10-6)*
1994**	XVII	Lillehammer, Norway	67	Norway, 26 (10-11-5)
1998	XVIII	Nagano, Japan		
2002	XIX	Salt Lake City, Utah		

* *One German team after reunification of East and West Germany in 1990.*

** *The IOC voted in 1988 to move the XVII Winter Games ahead two years in order to separate them from Summer Games and to alternate the two Olympics every two years.*

PARTICIPATION IN THE MODERN OLYMPICS

YEAR	SUMMER GAMES Athletes		WINTER GAMES Athletes	
	Male	Female	Male	Female
1896	311	–		
1900	1319	11		
1904	681	6		
1908	1999	36		
1912	2490	57		
1920	2543	64		
1924	2956	136	281	13
1928	2724	290	366	27
1932	1281	127	277	30
1936	3738	328	680	76
1948	3714	385	636	77
1952	4407	518	624	108
1956	3103	397	687	132
1960	4738	610	502	146
1964	4457	683	758	175
1968	4750	781	1063	230
1972	6659	1171	927	218
1976	4915	1274	1013	218
1980	4320	1192	1012	271
1984	5458	1620	1127	283
1988	6983	2438	1270	364
1992	7555	3008	1801	488
1994			1302	542
1996	(estimated 10,000)			

A.7

IMPROVEMENTS IN SELECTED SUMMER OLYMPIC RECORDS FOR MEN

Event	Mark in Year of Origin	Present Record	Improvement
Track			
Marathon	2 hr 58:50 (1896)	2, 09:21 (1984)	28%
110-m hurdles	17.6 sec (1896	12.98 (1988)	26%
1500-m	4 min 33.2 (1896)	3:32.53 (1984)	22%
800-m	2 min 11 (1896)	1:43 (1984)	21%
400-m	54.2 sec (1896)	43.5 (1992)	20%
400-m hurdles	57.6 sec (1900)	46.78 (1992)	19%
3000-m steeplechase	10 min 0.4 (1920)	8:05.51 (1988)	19%
100-m	12.0 sec (1896)	9.92 (1988)	17%
10,000-m	31 min 20.8 (1912)	27:21.46 (1988)	13%
400-m relay	42.4 sec (1912)	37.4 (1992)	12%
200-m	22.2 sec (1900)	19.75 (1988)	11%
5000-m	14 min 36.6 (1912)	13:05.59 (1984)	10%

*Average of improvements in 12 men's track events: **18%***

Event	Mark in Year of Origin	Present Record	Improvement
Field			
discus throw	95 ft 7 1/2 (1896)	225' 9 (1988)	136%
16-lb shot put	36 ft 9 3/4 (1896)	73' 8 3/4 (1988)	100%
pole vault	10 ft 10 (1896)	19' 9 1/4 (1988)	83%
javelin throw	179 ft 10 (1908)	310' 4 (1976)	73%
16 lb hammer throw	163 ft 1 (1900)	278' 2 (1988)	71%
long jump	20 ft 10 (1896)	29' 2 1/2 (1968)	40%
triple jump	44 ft 11 3/4 (1896)	59' 7 1/2 (1992)	33%
running high jump	5 ft 11 1/4 (1896)	7' 9 3/4 (1988)	32%

*Average of improvements in 8 men's field events: **71%***

Event	Mark in Year of Origin	Present Record	Improvement
Swimming			
100-m freestyle	1 min 22.2 (1896)	48.63 sec (1988)	41%
1500-m freestyle	22 min 48.4 (1908)	14 min 43.48 (1992)	35%
800-m freestyle relay	10 min 55.6 (1908)	7 min 11.95 (1992)	34%
400-m freestyle	5 min 36.8 (1908)	3 min 45 (1992)	33%
200-m breast stroke	3 min 9.2 (1908)	2 min 10.16 (1992)	31%
100-m backstroke	1 min 16.8 (1904)	53.98 sec (1992)	30%

*Average of improvements in 6 men's swimming events: **34%***

A.8

RECORD SETTING
IN SELECTED OLYMPIC EVENTS

	No. of Final Events*	World Records	Olympic Records Broken**
SUMMER GAMES			
MEN'S TRACK & FIELD 1896-1992	494	84 (17%)	261 (53%)
WOMEN'S TRACK & FIELD 1928-1992	173	40 (23%)	108 (62%)
MEN'S SWIMMING 1896-1992	198	79 (40%)	140 (71%)
WOMEN'S SWIMMING 1912-1992	154	52 (34%)	119 (77%)
WINTER GAMES			
MEN'S SPEED SKATING 1924-1992	69	11 (16%)	39 (57%)
WOMEN'S SPEED SKATING 1960-1992	38	6 (16%)	28 (74%)

*   *Includes only events in existence as of the 1992 Games.*
** *Includes both world records and the times when only the Olympic record was broken.*

A. 9

CURRENT OLYMPIC SPORTS
(AND YEAR INTRODUCED)

Summer Games

Archery (1900)
Athletics [Track & Field] (1896)
Badminton (1992)
Baseball (1992)
  Women's Softball (1996)
Basketball (1936)
Boxing (1904)
Canoe / Kayak (1936)
Cycling (1896)
  Mountain Cycling (1996)
Equestrian (1900)
Fencing (1896)
Field Hockey (1908)
Football [Soccer] (1900)
Gymnastics (1896)
Judo (1964)

Modern Pentathlon (1912)
Rowing (1900)
Shooting (1896)
Swimming (1896)
  Diving (1904)
  Synchronized Swimming (1984)
  Water Polo (1900)
Table Tennis (1988)
Team Handball (1972)
Tennis (1896; reintroduced 1988)
Volleyball (1964)
  Beach Volleyball (1996)
Weightlifting (1896)
Wrestling (1896)
Yachting (1896)*

Winter Games

Biathlon (1960)
Bobsled (1924)
Ice Hockey (1920/1924)
Luge (1964)

Skating, figure (1908/1920/1924)
Skating, speed (1924)
Skiing (1924)

* *Yachting was scheduled for the 1896 Games but was cancelled because of heavy seas.*

THE FOUR MAJOR PANHELLENIC FESTIVALS

FESTIVAL (in order of importance)	ORIGIN AND LOCATION	VICTORY WREATH
Olympian Games	From 776 B.C., honoring the chief god Zeus, at Olympia (held every four years in the first month after the summer solstice and marked the beginning of each four-year Olympiad)	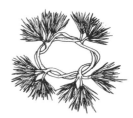 **wild olive**
Isthmian Games	From 523 B.C., said to be founded by the god of the sea Poseidon, at the Isthmus of Corinth (in the spring of every 2nd and 4th years of the Olympiad)	 **pine**
Pythian Games	From 527 B.C., honoring the god of the sun Apollo, at Delphi (in August - September of every 3rd year of the Olympiad)	 **laurel**
Nemean Games	From 516 B.C., in honor of Zeus, at Nemea (every 2nd and 4th years of the Olympiad)	**wild celery**

INDEX

Edd Wheeler graduated from the U.S. Air Force Academy in 1962 and served as a line officer. He is a federal administrative law judge and has held regional and national racquets titles. His experience in the law has afforded ample exposure to games and gaming.